SO-CBS-669

Writing
Science News
for the
Mass Media

Writing
Science News
for the
Mass Media

Second Edition, Revised

David Warren Burkett

Gulf Publishing Company
Houston, Texas

Library of Congress Catalog Card Number: 7284334

ISBN: 0-87201-924-1

Contents

Foreword   vii

Preface   ix

1   Introduction to Science Writing   1

2   Expanding Fields for Science Writing   7

3   What is Science News?   32

4   Writing Science News   58

5   Covering the Scientific Convention   81

6   Three Principles of Usefulness   103

7   Special Problems and Ethics   118

8   Science and Censorship   142

9   How to Write a Story   174

References   183

Appendix   199

    Awards   199

    Fellowships   206

    Science Writing Associations   208

Index   209

Foreword

Most newspaper editors today no longer hold with the naive journalistic fundamentalism that proclaims, "Any good reporter can cover any story." Nevertheless, newspaper readers should be impressed at the wide variety of subjects the best general reporter can handle successfully.

Unfortunately, science, medicine and technology are no longer among such subjects. Even a top reporter, if he or she lacks interest in and understanding of these fields, will usually botch stories on science, medicine or technology. Just as bad, the editor who thinks his general reporter can handle these topics will probably not recognize the mess the reporter has made nor understand the inevitable bitter complaints from scientists, physicians and engineers.

Today a slowly increasing number of editors realize that covering science, no less than reporting on sports, requires special knowledge. Although the paper may have a sports staff, it may feel it cannot afford a full-time science writer, but at least one or more general reporters can learn something of science and related fields.

In addition to knowledge of facts and latest developments in science, the reporter should be acquainted with peculiarities of covering science and the difficulties of dealing with its practitioners. Warren Burkett has applied his long personal experience and has mined his way through a vast literature in this successful effort to discuss these problems.

Here you can read about the ethical dilemmas of science writing; the coverage of large, jargon-filled, multisessioned scientific meetings; the ways science stories can be handled for greatest effectiveness. Should you check your story with a scientist before handing it in? You'll have to decide for yourself, but you can find here what experienced science writers do.

The official custodian of a large bibliographic file of articles, speeches, letters, pamphlets and other communications about science writing, I can attest to the fact that Mr. Burkett has condensed a great outpouring of thought and talk into relatively few pages. The wise professors at The University of Texas School of Journalism who permitted him to write this book as his thesis have done the whole enterprise of journalism a lasting favor.

Henry A. Goodman
Executive Secretary,
Council for the Advancement
of Science Writing

Leonia, New Jersey
December, 1971

Preface

Studies which made this report possible began under the sponsorship of the School of Communication at The University of Texas and Columbia University's Graduate School of Journalism. Their continuation was encouraged by William P. Steven, while editor of *The Houston Chronicle,* and by the managers of McGraw-Hill's World News. My thanks go to DeWitt C. Reddick and Norris G. Davis of Texas and to John Foster, now retired as director of Columbia's Advanced Science Writing Program, for their advice and assistance.

I am indebted also to fellow science writers for their time, speeches, writings and comments about this demanding specialty in the profession of journalism. They have responded magnificently to the challenges of the sciences, their readers and their media over three decades of turbulent change.

The assistance of Houston Endowment Inc., John T. Jones and other trustees is gratefully acknowledged; they and the Council for the Advancement of Science Writing have made possible the presentation of academic work, in pursuit of a masters degree, in a form useful to practicing journalists.

Thanks also to Gay Burkett, my wife, and to my children, Karl and Patricia. I shall forever owe them a debt of gratitude for their help and unselfish cooperation over the years.

David Warren Burkett

May, 1972
Washington, D.C.

1

Introduction to Science Writing

The New Role of Science in the News

The growing importance of science in creating news and timely information is a striking development in modern journalism with evidence available on every hand. For instance, consider these following recent examples of developments related to science and the news.

Scientists assemble the first, crude synthetic genes and enzymes; their announcement touches off a controversy over the potential of this discovery to heal man's ills or control his psyche.

Physicists tell Congress their technical judgment does not support the feasibility or desirability of building a complex federal antiballistic missile defense.

Americans land on the moon, first men to set foot on land outside their own planet; while scientists probe the secrets in samples of rocks from the moon, more engineers prepare for manned and unmanned flights to other planets.

Four students die at the hands of National Guardsmen during a campus riot. and a science writer interviews physiologists who report that lack of sleep may have impaired judgment in both groups (179).

1

Congress wrestles with approval of a treaty banning nuclear weapons tests; the issue affects a presidential election. On election eve, two prominent scientists argue for the test moratorium saying "a Soviet military technologist, writing from the point of view of the U.S.S.R., could write an almost identical paper."

Developments in the transplantation of human hearts and in the design of artificial hearts pose not only technical and medical problems, but they raise grave social, ethical and economic issues as well. This is true of almost all organ replacement and substitution advancements. In fact, one of the enduring debates which will occupy thoughtful people for many decades is "technological assessment." This is the not-so-easy process of attempting to forecast the long-range effects of new inventions upon man and his social and physical world. As two landmark studies by the National Academy of Sciences and the National Academy of Engineering point out (163, 164), it will be no simple debate.

Until 1970, prevailing opinion of their fellows absolved individual scientists and engineers from responsibility for specific applications of their discoveries and inventions. Victor Cohn, science editor of *The Washington Post,* caught the shift of mood toward acceptance of both professional and individual responsibility (56). This will put the scientists and their professional societies more squarely into politics than before. Until now, political participation by scientists was evident mainly in presidential election years. Almost routinely scientists, engineers and doctors were recruited to lend their names to local, regional and national panels supporting one candidate or the other. Until the Nixon administration, however, professional standing, not politics, generally determined appointments to the top posts in scientific or technical agencies. This situation changed in 1969.

Then the White House rejected one man proposed as director of the National Science Foundation. Because the candidate opposed policy on the Vietnam conflict, even the endorsement of the President's science advisor was overridden. Outrage expressed by the scientific community brought a formal apology from President Richard Nixon—but the scientist never got the NSF job.

Nearly 400 drugs in common use were found useless or danger-ous by investigators working for the National Academy of Sciences. Removal of these drugs from the market, under orders of the Food and Drug Administration, will take years. The cost of manufacturers will come to many millions of dollars. Similarly, the company which develops an effective new drug may expect to make millions. So the science writer touches material of great social, political and economic importance.

Alton Blakeslee, respected science writer for the Associated Press, was offered nearly $17,000 to mention a commercial drug in one of his stories. Most of this sum, Blakeslee reported, was to be paid secretly and indirectly by the drug manufacturer (59:60).

The question of how much detail the human eye can resolve (visual acuity) has long intrigued a variety of physical and biolo-gical scientists. Research in this area entered a new dimension in the space flight era when scientists painted huge "eye charts" on the Texas desert beneath the astronauts' flight path (46:12).

Organized literature in journalism and science contains very little about the men and women operating between science in public affairs and the citizen. These few examples illustrate some of the powerful links between those who call themselves "scien-tists" and the mass of our individual citizens through our public life. Science no longer hides behind the closed doors of a labora-tory. It has become a part of the tough-and-tumble existence of the political, economic and cultural world.

With the changing role of science, it became apparent that the 1960s would see an expansion of science writers, particularly those belonging to the National Association of Science Writers (NASW).

Many NASW members are scientists who spend much of their time speaking and writing to the public. Declared a publication of the NASW:

The science writer, then, may be a newspaper reporter; a television script-writer; the public relations officer of a government research agency; the science editor of a laboratory research center and so on [84:2].

In the 1960s new educational programs for science writers were launched by universities and associations of writers. Recruiting drives expanded the NASW, the Aviation/Space Writers' Association and the American Medical Writers' Association. The National Science Foundation (NSF) and other agencies spent tens of thousands of dollars to acquaint journalists with science and scientists. The National Aeronautics and Space Administration (NASA) operates under a strong legal directive to spread public understanding of its science and engineering programs.

Earl J. Johnson, retired vice-president and editor of United Press International, tells of shifting from a bloody railroad strike to coverage of a science convention. The biggest "news" story, by judgment of the reporters then, was how scientists changed the sex of a chicken with hormone injections.

"No doubt I was a versatile fellow. But it was a superficial versatility neither wire service would tolerate now," Johnson said at the Sixteenth Annual William Allen White Memorial Lecture.

Newspaper subscribers are more mature now, he said, and both wire services must recognize that "labor and science and even horse racing require reporters with special qualifications" (112:11).

Purpose of This Book

The rapidly enlarging scope of science in the news has caused the demand for competent science writers to exceed the supply. Efforts are being made to draft writers from general reporting, acquainting them as quickly as possible with science in action. This guidebook to science writing may enable a student or professional writer to accelerate his transition into science writing.

The book examines the scope and objectives of science writing for a nonscientific audience. In doing so, the author has pulled together scattered references to the functions of the science writer, drawing upon books, articles, speeches and the writers' own professional discussion. This study, in part, pictures the science writer in action. It attempts to provide some partial answers to such questions as: What is science news? When does scientific experimenting become newsworthy? At what point does scientific development become involved in political action? Who are the science writers? How do they gather their material? What do they do with it? What are their relations with the scientists? How do they stand with fellow journalists in terms of their pay, their experience and their approach to their job? How do they attempt to improve their performance?

This discussion will summarize some of the principles of science writing which have become commonly accepted by leaders in the field. It will devote attention to the responsibilities of the science writer and to the ethical problems which confront him in certain situations. Particularly, it will examine questions involving national security or "pseudo-security" clouded by censorship.

Procedures

The book leans heavily on the running dialogue between scientists and writers in the weekly magazine *Science,* the quarterly *Newsletter* of the National Association of Science Writers and the transcripts of symposia devoted to communication, science and medicine. The references document and illustrate points of the discussion, observations of the author and suggestions of his fellow science writers. Readers will find mention of books and other materials commonly used by professional science writers as sources of news and background information in science and medicine.

Some of the techniques of combating governmental secrecy were adapted by the writer to meet challenges posed by the science-oriented agencies. Most of these techniques have been used by newsmen to gain access to public records and public officials. Thus, these approaches to science writing cannot be considered entirely new and untested.

Keeping Current

Some readers may fret about lack of emphasis on "how-to-do-it" instructions. Writing is a highly individualistic enterprise, and

variety in style, subject matter and approach should receive en-
couragement in every way. Case studies and examples of how
practicing science writers approach their writing and research
abound in this book. They should provide the writer a start for his
own work. Exploring the materials listed in the bibliography will
expand the writer's understanding of this specialty.

For those who wish to follow a reading program devoted to
the many approaches in preparing news, feature, radio and television material, libraries and bookstores contain detailed textbooks
for guidance. Writers also keep up to date on the changing needs
of editors by watching what these editors publish and broadcast.
Another guide, and a "tip-sheet" for ideas as well, is the *Clipsheet*,
a selection of science articles reproduced by the National Association of Science Writers.

2
Expanding Fields for Science Writing

It would be easy to believe that public interest in science began with the atomic bomb. To do so, however, ignores thousands of years in which mankind has struggled to understand the physical world and man's place in it. The writer or editor misleads himself if he believes that new information about the natural world interests only a few professional people who call themselves "scientists."

Awareness of the importance of the physical and biological sciences is coupled to varying degrees of ignorance about its mechanics. The American president and the Russian premier, however, do not waste words justifying a call for international cooperation in scientific and medical projects or a boast of national pride in the accomplishments of their scientists. Constituencies in both countries have watched the scientists' understanding of natural laws adapted to produce a technology which, in social terms, affects jobs, money, education and creature comforts. The changes wrought by science, engineering and technology have accelerated so rapidly that they have outstripped the public's ability to prepare for many of the changes and the writers' ability to grasp and explain the implications of these changes. The attempt to understand a changing world creates new opportunities for science writers.

Don K. Price of the John F. Kennedy School of Government, holds that America's faith in the marriage of science and democracy has been shaken by the problems of depressions and wars. To him, this represents a reversal of political opinion from the days of Benjamin Franklin and Thomas Jefferson. Russians have retained this faith and preach throughout Asia and Africa that the Communist system is now the only political approach grounded on scientific method (192:745).

Such a shift in opinion likely helped produce the political climate variously regarded as "anti-science" or "anti-intellectual" of the late 60s and early 70s. However, the cost of U.S. involvement in Vietnam produced a genuine imbalance in economic demands.

Where Has Science Gone?

There was, no doubt, less direct public awareness of science and scientists when research was confined to a small corner of the university. Now, however, the increased activity of scientists has expanded into areas of official and public concern. Nowhere is this expansion more apparent than in the military establishment.

Civilian and military laymen may only generally understand the scientific principles of many modern weapons. However, the declaration of a scientist that his associates cannot contact military planners brings immediate reaction. Congressmen threaten investigations, and there are charges that the planning of new weapons may be delayed unless the scientists talk directly with defense planners (213:2). There is a painful awareness that the atomic and hydrogen bombs, the heat-seeking infrared missiles and the intercontinental rockets burst from scientific laboratories into deadly hardware. Like Pandora's box, the laboratory of basic and applied science appears capable of producing new surprises in weaponry.

Industrial nations require close participation of scientists in policy matters. The president, as commander-in-chief, requires scientific advisors for his personal staff at international arms control negotiations and on special study commissions formed to recommend policies dealing with the environment, pollution, education and with science itself (190).

The most thorough basic studies of science and technology in national governments have been carried out by the Organization for Economic Cooperation and Development, based in Paris. Its *Reviews of National Science Policy: United States* presents the only comprehensive view of the structure of scientific effort within the U.S. government (177).

The precise architecture of science-in-government has been rearranged by shifts in the bureaucracy, but this study remains the most thorough look at how a government organizes for scientific endeavor.

Science's economic importance can be counted also in dollars and cents. The National Science Foundation issues regular reports on the share of funds devoted to science within the economy, the federal budget and private industry. In this decade, for example, research and development receives over $30 billion annually, about 3 percent of the gross national product. Industry's share has climbed to more than $16.4 billion as the share of federal support dropped from 59 to 51 percent. The United States contains more than 500,000 full-time scientists and engineers in all fields, and about 387,000 work in industry where 70 percent of all research and development (R&D) work is actually done (170). This figure is heavily biased by costs attributable to space and defense hardware development. Expenses for fundamental research and exploratory engineering, the equivalent in applied science to basic research, accounts for only about $700 million in industry. Most of this basic activity takes place in universities, in federal contract research centers operated for government by business and in nonprofit research foundations (168). More than 2,000 universities and colleges receive federal research and development support, amounting to nearly $1.4 billion annually (167).

Thus, science technology and engineering (often called *applied science* in contrast to *pure science*) tackle and solve problems while creating others. As in the atomic bomb development, answering one set of problems never guarantees, even in peaceful fields, that the solution will not create new problems.

The questions go beyond how many present workers may be replaced by machines operated on "information" fed from computers. Labor columnist Victor Riesel now writes about men who assemble spaceships and about the potential miners and processors of minerals yet to be discovered on moons and planets yet to be visited (201:32). Specialists in labor and economics must attempt to estimate what new labor forces must be trained and organized. Union members and the sons of members may see in the unraveling of nature's secrets what future jobs they may hold.

Moving atomic fission from the laboratory into the battlefield weds the scientist forever to government and politics. "This was inevitable from the day the Manhattan Project was initiated," said H. Bentley Glass, professor of biology at Johns Hopkins University (85:603). The wedding has, in the national interest, limited international exchanges between scientists. The laws governing classified information are strict. Many scientists, with Dr. Glass, think the price has been paid by science itself.

> As every scientist knows, the free interplay of thoughts between minds far outstrips in productivity the isolated, clonal generation of ideas, even by a genius [85:603].

Financial rewards have been great. As noted by Dr. Glass, the typical research scientist of 1940 had a budget of $100, a Sears and Roebuck pressure cooker for a sterilizer and a dusty but cool basement for a laboratory. He spent 80 percent of his time teaching and taking care of university chores. Twenty years later the same scientist could run two research labs with a federally supported staff of six and spend a budget of $50,000 or more.

Don K. Price gave a wry recognition to the scientists' new political power:

A mere two decades ago, federal support of science in private institutions was a distant dream. Today it is an established political habit—indeed a vested interest. If I may yield to the dangerous temptation of using a scientist's term as a political metaphor, I suspect that research as a political force has already attained its critical mass. It may not yet be a farm bloc. But there are enough people and institutions directly interested in it, and enough people persuaded of its importance, so that I doubt that even the sudden outbreak of peace on earth and good will in Moscow would have as much effect on our research as on our military budget [193:764].

Expansion of scientific activity, coupled to politics and government, crosses national and international interests. This should not be confused with science's traditional international exchange of information. This new internationality involves coordinated, multinational research assaults upon scientific problems. Over the next decade, science writers will be reporting on such projects as the Global Atmospheric Research Program (GARP) and the International Biological Program (IBP). GARP covers a diverse number of small and large efforts to fill gaps in man's knowledge about the air and ocean. With luck, scientists will acquire enough data on the world-wide relationships of land, sea and air phenomena to make two-week weather forecasts with an accuracy comparable to present three-day forecasts. IBP deals with ecology on a broad scale.

Such ambitious programs are relatively new. They began with the International Geophysical Year (IGY) of 1957-58; a small part of IGY blossomed with Russia's successful Sputnik launching into space exploration, which took on a separate life of its own. IGY was followed in 1961 by a 20-nation effort to explore the Indian Ocean as a potential food source. And in 1964-65, the International Quiet Sun Year (IQSY) focused scientific studies upon the sun during a period when sunspot activity was at a minimum. Most international efforts are coordinated for the United States through the foreign secretary of the National Academy of Sciences. The Academy acts for, and in concert with, the scientific advisors of the U.S. Department of State.

The influence of federal funds on scientific activity makes the federal budget a relevant scientific document each year. Scientific research and development money is scattered throughout the federal budget. Therefore a special analysis document is drawn each year by the president's advisors to focus attention on these and other fields such as education, social sciences, environment, etc. (36:257). For scientists and science writers, these economic documents forecast the trends of scientific research in the immediate and long-term future.

The dollar position in a proposed federal budget does not necessarily predict the end-point in the game. For example, Victor Cohn of *The Washington Post* noted that the National Science Foundation was approaching a genuine milestone in 1970, after many years of seeking an actual appropriation from Congress of over $500 million (54).

State governments employ nearly 88,000 scientists, engineers and technicians. Although their numbers are increasing, relatively few show up in research and development work outside the state universities. State agencies spend less than $100 million for research and development, about 10 percent of the total state expenditures. Nearly 80 percent of state research and development funds is used for health, hospitals, natural resources and highways. Health and life sciences dominate the disciplines used in state governments (168).

For the science writer, these statisics give him a frame of reference for the economic, social, political and cultural significance of the people whose work supplies the information from which he fashions his stories and his broadcasts. However, they are a part of his audience; unless he writes for a specialized scientific or industrial journal, they are not the mass of his audience. The National Science Foundation estimate of 350,000 persons holding doctorate degrees in science by 1980 means that millions will have greater science literacy than ever before.

Prof. Hillier Krieghbaum, chairman of the National Association of Science Writers survey committee, sees a hopeful time ahead for science popularization because the readership of science news increases directly with the number of science courses readers take in high school and college (129:1093).

Economic awareness of the scientific explosion is inescapable. Industry employs more than 300,000 engineers and 100,000 scientists. Doctors of science head some of the country's largest firms. There are 30,000 industrial research laboratories, each staffed to bring basic and applied science into the marketplace to justify the expenditure of corporate funds for research and development. E.I. du Pont de Nemours Company officials estimate that 75 percent of the company profits comes from products which were in research laboratories only 10 years ago. Sharing in these profits has made millionaires out of several scientists (151:96).

Business writers must study products and finance in the light of scientific developments. Research expansion means new jobs paying higher than average salaries.

The electronics, automation, computation, petrochemical, plastics and missile industries have moved laboratory curiosities swiftly into common usage. Yet the nature of thermoelectricity was known more than 100 years ago, as John Johnsrud of *The New York Times* had to explain when writing about new refrigerators, freezers and electric generators entering the market (114:43).

Neither the science writer nor the business writer can ignore ways in which the science-engineering-technology expansion arouses social tension. Electronic computers in 10 years developed into one of the most important stories in business. They are credited with making America the first country in history to increase productivity while the number of its productive workers declined (50).

Agricultural scientists breed plant varieties for stems, foliage and fruit characteristics that favor machine harvesting. Engineers and technicians improve and increase the number of machines capable of gathering and processing crops in the fields. Will the social and economic problems of the migratory laborer and his children be solved by training the migrant to work the machines, as suggested by the President's Committee on Migratory Labor (110:46), or will this marginal economic activity cease?

In 1962, President John F. Kennedy challenged Premier Nikita Khrushchev to a cooperative U.S.-U.S.S.R. space program. This action expanded the presidency to include "chief scientist" among its holder's many roles. This role has been emphasized in varying degrees by men in the office, but none has abandoned it. Indeed, it was President Richard Nixon who actually initiated just such a space program—and other programs—with Russia in 1972.

Journalists should not confuse this kind of international cooperative effort toward a shared goal with international efforts pursued along strictly individual and national lines. As noted by Rudy Abramson of the *Los Angeles Times,* the work of controlling the hydrogen bomb's fusion process to produce thermoelectric power is pursued by Russia and the United States along national lines; exchange of information takes place freely at a technical but informal level (5).

Changing Role of the Scientist

New roles have also been thrust upon scientists. These derive partly from public trust accompanying the acceptance of public money, from the need for more leadership and coordination and from the size and cost of scientific undertakings.

An emerging figure is the political or even the "pork-barrel" scientist. The biography of Dr. Harold Brown noted that he was a Democrat when he was appointed director of research and engineering in the Department of Defense and an active campaigner for President Kennedy (184:8). Many other political appointments can be found, as contrasted with civil service appointments calling for professional skills alone.

From trusted political positions in government, scientists can function in other dimensions. As a case in point, President Kennedy was credited with using scientists as personal emissaries to secure the release of American Air Force officers imprisoned after their reconnaissance plane was shot down by Russians (279:1).

As reported, the first step to secure the fliers' release was made in Moscow by Dr. Walt W. Rostow, later deputy assistant to the president for national security, and Dr. Jerome B. Wiesner, the president's scientific advisor. The scientists dealt directly with Soviet Foreign Office personnel rather than indirectly through Russian scientists in similar government positions. The Americans were in Russia for the sixth annual Pugwash Conference of Scientists and Scholars.

Scientists also battle over the national interest and ideology at meetings of the International Atomic Energy Agency of the United Nations (107).

When stakes are both political and scientific, scientists "play the game." Until the Nixon administration, politics was considered very much subordinate to scientific competence and respect of fellow scientists. Dr. John S. Foster, Jr., for example, served as the chief of military R&D programs under Democrat Lyndon B. Johnson and Republican Nixon.

However, in the Nixon administration scientists' positions on nonscientific issues became a very important factor in appointments to positions in science-oriented agencies. The White House, for example, in 1969 turned down the scientist recommended by the president's science advisor and an agency policy board to head the National Science Foundation. The man had opposed official policy on Vietnam. Such protest arose from the scientific community that the president personally apologized to the NSF advisory board and to scientists generally. However, the job went to another man. Later the president rejected the recommendation of his own secretary of Health, Education and Welfare for a man to run the health and scientific programs of the department. Opposition by the American Medical Association to the man's ideas about pay and delivery of health services brought another scientist-administrator to the job after a long dispute.

As might be expected, the heat of political debate can lead normally cautious scientists and engineers to stretch facts to fit their causes. Scientists were deeply involved on both sides of the question of whether or not to build an anti-ballistic missile defense system. The scientists' interpretations and assumptions produced such widely varying recommendations that the Operations Research Society of America undertook a 21-month study to discover why. The society's committee on professional standards examined formal testimony, public letters to newspapers, advertisements, signed essays and other material published by the opposed witnesses. Both groups were found to have overstated their cases. However, the opponents of the system were criticised for being farther away from professional standards for scientific analysis.

The scientists exhibit no inclination, however, to deal themselves out. As one of the political scientists, the late Norbert Weiner declared, "Any scientist, participating in what has become a moving crap game, must expect to get slugged occasionally" (185:130).

Americans elected the first research scientist to Congress in 1964. Rep. Weston E. Vivian, holder of a Ph.D. degree in engineering, spent most of his time in research before entering Detroit politics. He failed to win a second term. Mike McCormack, with a masters degree in chemistry, spent 20 years as a research scientist and administrator at the Hanford, Washington, nuclear energy center. His scientific career was mixed with service in both houses of the Washington state legislature before he was elected to the U.S. House of Representatives in 1970.

Dr. Polykarp Kusch, Nobel laureate in physics, has characterized the debate over fallout as the result of political positions taken by many scientists from differing interpretation of scientific data (132). This or a similar controversy could provide the issue on which an election rests.

Accompanying the changing role of the scientist in the society has been his acceptance of a new responsibility to report to the society which sustains his activity. In some cases these reports fulfill legal requirements under government contracts. But more and more the scientist seeks public understanding. One manifestation of this is increased cooperation with the press. However, it should be said that this cooperation was desired more by the press than by many scientists.

Scientists cooperate with reporters by appearing for press conferences at scientific conventions. Scientists have served as educators of science writers at seminars arranged by the American Institute of Physics, among others. Here the scientists devote their time to informing reporters, and sometimes editors, about vital aspects of newsworthy research. For scientific conventions, scientists prepare or approve nontechnical versions of their papers. These are available at pressrooms set up at an increasing number of scientific meetings. The scientist has become more willing to grant private interviews to the general reporter as well as to the scientific or technical writer on a specialized publication. Often scientists speak directly to the public as authors and lecturers.

Reports from science writers who have attended European science meetings indicate that the cooperation between scientists and newsmen has not become as close there as in the United States. European scientific meetings provide simultaneous translations in many languages as the papers are presented, but there are usually no formal pressrooms and conferences. Interviews with scientists must be arranged individually by writers.

Changing Role of Science Writers

Expanded public awareness of science has also changed the role of the science writers. In 1938 only 11 reporters attended the convention of the American Association for the Advancement of Science in Richmond, Virginia. Twenty-three years later the AAAS meeting drew 362 representatives of the press, television and radio (171:489). Requests came from 42 countries for nontechnical abstracts of papers. The late Sidney S. Negus, the pressroom director, arranged 17 press conferences, two news programs, 11 network radio broadcasts, 14 network television programs, three regional telecasts and 22 taped interviews foradio.

In 1934 the National Association of Science Writers was formed with 12 members. Now the NASW has more than 750 members working for newspapers, magazines, wire services, radio and television, book publishers, universities, pharmaceutical houses, industrial laboratories and other organizations as well as those on a free-lance or independent basis (29). The American Medical Writers Association, with headquarters in New York has about 1,500 members (274:1).

The pioneer science writers were trained in the ways of journalism and acquired their scientific knowledge as part of their work and personal interests. The early members of the NASW included William L. Laurence of *The New York Times,* Robert D. Potter of the Medical Society of the County of New York, Watson Davis of Scripps-Howard Newspapers and Science Service, Allen Schoenfield of *The Detroit News,* Gobind Behari Lal of International News Service, Howard Blakeslee of the Associated Press, John J. O'Neill of *The New York Herald Tribune,* Delos Smith of United Press International, Waldemar Kaempffert of *The New York Times* and David Dietz of Scripps-Howard and the *Cleveland Press.*

Theirs was a mutual pioneering job with the scientists. As reporters they developed the technique of translating scientific reports into stories and submitting them to the scientists for checking. At the same time they taught scientists to trust the accuracy and balance of news writers (99:366). During this same period of the 1930s, Robert Dwyer of The New York Daily News and the City Press Association performed similar missionary work among the doctors and medical researchers at Bellevue Hospital (98). In recognition of their work, O'Neill, Laurence, Blakeslee, Lal and Dietz received 1937 Pulitzer Prizes for reporting. Members of NASW in the 1970s include an increasing number of men and women whose training includes the sciences. Partly this reflects the rising levels of science in formal education and the lucrative returns from an increased interest in science and medicine.

Pierre C. Fraley, former executive secretary for the Council for the Advancement of Science Writing, found one-third of the younger NASW members (20 to 29) had emphasized science courses in prepation for science writing careers (78:323). The majority of members, however, entered science writing through journalistic training: liberal arts, schools of journalism, the newspaper city room and assignment by their editor. Their education in science and medicine expands constantly through personal contact with scientists, by reading books and periodicals devoted to science, by attending science meetings and sometimes by formal classwork after working hours. Science writers also attend short courses sponsored by the NSF, the American Cancer Society and the American Institute of Physics, among others. Government and industry use a time-tried journalistic institution to improve the education of the science writer. This is the "junket." Junkets involve taking writers to a center of governmental or commercial activity the sponsor desires to publicize.

The United States regularly invites journalists to research stations in Antarctica, for instance. All the services transport science writers to bases where the services maintain research and development facilities. Experimenters usually are available to explain their work.

Among the very first women to reach Antarctica this way was Jean Pearson, science and aerospace writer for *The Detroit News* and president of the National Association of Science Writers. "On what other beat would you legitimately make the 20,000-mile round trip to the South Pole?" she asked on her return.

In recognition of the varying roles of science writers, the NASW maintains five classes of membership. One class is honorary. Active members engage in preparing and interpreting science news to the public or in "dissemination of accurate information regarding science through all media normally devoted to informing the public" (60:4). Associate and affiliate membership in the NASW opens for those who prepare science information but who do not meet the requirements of time or occupation that qualify for active membership. These associates usually do not write directly to the public. The division includes college and university teachers and public relations personnel.

Publicity writers, public relations personnel and information officers of industry and government compose a group of writers who translate scientific material into popular reading and listening matter and assist professional journalists in preparing such material. Business and industry employ as many science information writers in the publicity or information offices as management feels is necessary to promote understanding and acceptance of the organization's products. These persons help writers gather general and specific information and arrange interviews. It should be recognized that the company science writer's purpose is to protect his company's interest in science, medical and technical areas. Where the company deals with government and military contracts, information personnel also help interpret science and technology to an essentially nontechnical audience of congressmen and other federal officials.

Other employment opportunities for science writers can be found in schools, colleges and universities. Translators of science and technology are particularly useful for schools whose reputation and financing depend on public support of research work. Research foundations and institutions, organizations of professional scientists and many fund-raising groups depend on public understanding of science and medicine to enlist public support. The Sloan-Kettering Institute for Cancer Research, the American Cancer Society, the National Foundation and the American Heart Association all employ science and medical writers in their information departments.

One of the major generators of science news is the U.S. government. It is also one of the biggest employers of science and medical writers with varying degrees of competence. Military and civil service writers release information on government research from all levels within the establishment. Extremely active government agencies include the National Institutes of Health, the U.S. Public Health Service, the Atomic Energy Commission, the National Aeronautics and Space Administration, the Department of Defense research and development branches in each service, the Department of Commerce, the Environmental Protection Agency and the National Science Foundation. The U.S. Information Agency, restricted from distributing its material inside the country, hires science specialists at home and abroad to write news stories and broadcast material about American science for overseas audiences.

Expanding science establishments, better education and short-ened communication times have helped make science news imme-diate and plentiful. Newspapers and other media employ science specialists to develop local science news coverage and to help sift science stories from the literature, wire service reports and other sources of news gathering.

The increasing use of specialists stems in part from what J. Edward Murray of *The Detroit Free Press* calls a "crisis of mean-ing" (160:7). This demands better reporting more depth and pers-pective, better selection of stories and more science, economics and religion to replace more perishable news. It requires better personnel in terms of training, education and salary. John Hohen-berg, professor at Columbia's Graduate School of Journalism, sees the specialist arising from greater public interest in science—and from increased competition between media (99:366). Newspapers must throw human and financial resources against the claims of television, radio and magazines upon the reader's time.

In an instant world of powdered coffee, space trips and swift crises, the specialist supplies "instant background" in the field of science. Other and older specialties have existed in the newspapers in the fields of sports, politics, courts, business and entertainment. Newer areas of specialization have included the military, education and urban planning or business writers as well as the closely re-lated trilogy of space, science and medicine. The time writers devote to these specialties ranges from full-time to a few hours weekly.

The close relationship between science and medicine often makes it impractical to distinguish between the two in staffing a conference of scientists and physicians. Wire service science writers move from medical convention to science convention. Earl Ubell of WCBS-TV News writes freely in both fields. However, *The Houston Chronicle, The Houston Post* and *The Philadelphia Bulle-tin,* among others, assign different individuals to science and medi-cine. By-lines in *The New York Times* indicate a preference not only to keep certain writers generally on science or medicine stor-ies but also to switch them into new areas regularly.

Specialized reporters, says Hohenberg, do not usually "come green from the campuses" (99:365). Editors want minimum competence in all newspaper skills before giving any specialist the run of his particular field.

The burgeoning of science leads Walter Sullivan, news editor of *The New York Times* science reporters, to emphasize the choice which he must make between a true news story about science on the one hand and business, feature or general news stories on the other. "There the criterion is whether or not the subject matter requires a scientific background to be covered properly," Sullivan writes (241). On the clearly scientific story there is no problem, he finds, and judgments may be made on the merits as science news. How new is it? How important? How interesting to the general reader? *The New York Times,* with its wealth of personnel, routes the science staff's copy through editors who have a special interest in science.

Science: Secondary Component of News

Newspapers, radio, television and magazines distribute much science news while dealing with other stories. This information about science and medicine is a secondary, but vital, component of the news on any particular day. Understanding the news may hinge upon the reporter's understanding of this secondary technical information.

Illnesses and the assassination of public figures have kept hundreds of science and medical writers searching anatomy books and consulting local and national experts. The news, of course, is the event—the illness of presidents, such as Eisenhower or Johnson, or the assassination of President John F. Kennedy and his brother, Senator Robert F. Kennedy, a candidate for the presidency. After the event, however, it is the science writer who stands closest in background and experience to the professionals who can best explain the medical implications of the event and answer such vital questions as, "Will he survive; what are his chances? Can he perform the functions of his office?"

The growth of science also catches the local writer. The general reporter, the education writer and often the women's news reporter must deal with a phenomenon known as "the science fair." Thousands of such fairs are held annually in elementary, junior high and high schools. Reporters find themselves confronted with homemade atom smashers, "double-blind" tests and the mechanics of "neutron decay" and "autoimmunization".

Enough samples are in hand to raise the question of what scientific information the newspaper presents to the parents and fellow classmates of science fair exhibitors. The answer often is *none*. Rarely does the reader expand his own knowledge of science by reading about the activities of these youngsters. Rarely does he get an explanation of the scientific problem the student tackled, how he went about it and why the winning exhibits surpassed others in the show. Too often general reporters think it is somehow more interesting to brush off the science fair with the idea that what the youngsters do is wonderful, amazing, complicated and "Ha, Ha, we don't understand a bit of it."

Police reporters often get involved with science and medical stories relating to crime, violence and other police business. For instance, a story about a diabetic jailed and his condition neglected because police think him a common drunk would call for an explanation of the disease and its effects as well as how the event was allowed.

Rising violence in the past few years, the increase of riotous demonstrations, the social separation often called the "generation gap" and the introduction of new research programs of crime control and law enforcement have brought science writers more deeply into stories about crime, criminals and other social problems. They have expanded from the traditional literature of physics, chemistry and biology into that of sociology, psychology and other behavioral sciences. They have drawn upon new experts, including the staff of such centers as that for the study of violence at Brandeis University.

Henry A. Goodman, executive secretary of the Council for the Advancement of Science Writing, has helped meet the new demands. CASW has organized seminars focused upon the social sciences and their contributions toward solving current problems of the alienated, the poor, the minorities, the urban and suburban citizen.

Social scientists have not been ecstatic over the treatment of their material (288). On the other hand, John Wykert found speakers at an American Psychoanalytic Association meeting palming off "elderly, 'textbook' material" on science writers invited to a special APA seminar. He felt that the only reason for holding the seminar was to stir up publicity that might increase the number of applicants for training in analysis (284). *Society*, edited at Rutgers University, attempts to publish significant new social science studies in a semipopular style; it is a valuable story source for mass media writers. So is *Psychology Today*. The major news magazines have established departments for stories from the behaviorial sciences. Philip Meyer, one of the few journalists with formal social science training, was used by the Knight Newspapers to coordinate a field study of Detroit rioters; teams from Wayne State and Michigan State universities interviewed more than 400 people under his direction (155).

Rapid social change, sociologists predict, will equal that of the physical sciences after World War II. Such social flux may prove extremely traumatic and sharpen the mass media's need for social science specialists. Premature attempts to apply social science research on a broad scale certainly will provoke controversy, as physician Arnold Hutschnecker, M.D., discovered. He proposed using an experimental screening test to spot potential lawbreakers among children six to eight years old; those who flunked would be sent to federal clinics for continuing therapy. After all the major social science professional associations announced their opposition, the Department of Health, Education and Welfare buried the proposal (69).

Dr. Amitai Etzioni of Columbia University has proposed creating a field of "macrosociology" to train professionals specifically to become editors, journalists and political scientists.

Mass Media and Violence, one of the volumes produced by the National Commission on the Causes and Prevention of Violence (Government Printing Office, 1970), is indispensable for any writer translating social science research for popular reading.

Reporters of governmental affairs face tremendous problems studying contracts awarded on the basis of "good science." Does the reporter know what is "good science"? Can he act as a watchdog of public funds as, for instance, he does in observing the expense accounts of congressmen traveling overseas? Can the reporter recognize "conflict of interest" when scientific advisors assign research grants to university science departments or medical schools which supply one or more advisors?

Higher education and research, particularly scientific research, are inextricably woven together, observed Gerard Piel, publisher of *Scientific American* (185:205). The education writer must consider the training given students at all levels; he must have an interest in what skills are being taught, as must the labor writer. Several science writers, as well as education and general reporters, have found state textbooks in biology, physics and other areas far behind current developments.

In tracing the flow of the news, one gains the impression that balanced reporting of the world and local science requires consideration of what scientists' research can add to events of this age. This view gains confirmation from a study of a list of 100 events that the editors of *The New York Times* believed most significant in 1961 (176:6E). Fourteen stories were based on scientific research and development. None of them, including those of the effects of fallout or the detection of nuclear tests, could be called exclusively "science news" covered exclusively by science or medical reporters. On the other hand, the science writers devoted many stories to the scientific aspects of these 14 news stories.

The gross statistics raise a question, however. How many newspapers, magazines, wire services or television stations could give 14 percent of the staff's man-hours to communication of information verified from the scientific community? Too often, it appears, such information arrives far behind the news event.

Control Centers of News Coverage

The question of how manpower is allocated seems crucial. M.W. Thistle, public information officer for the National Research Council of Canada, argues that the decision makers on newspapers seldom have any idea of the time, background and study needed to produce a good item of science; neither do they move among scientists to the degree they move among the political, economic or social leaders (254:458).

However, these decision makers sit in the operational and policy control centers of communications media where they allocate personnel and money. Each newspaper, wire service, magazine or radio-television station had a finite and usually predetermined amount of space and time. Men and women in these control centers must allocate the use of this space and time. These people carry various titles and specific duties. In a rough analogy common to newspapers, the controllers include the publisher, executive editor, news editor, city editor and their assistants. Some, such as the city and news editors, determine the assignment of writers to particular stories each day.

In addition, individual deskmen and copy editors read, edit, trim and headline each story. Their activities also influence the quantity and quality of scientific information which reaches the public. The intended purpose of the editorial desks is to assure the accuracy of the information published. However, some of the most bitter words against science news in the popular press have been hurled at work performed by headline writers and copy editors. Although these copy editors probably catch some inaccuracies, the number of complaints traceable directly to desk operations indicate the need for some deeper understanding of science news by individual editors.

Another control center is the wire or telegraph editor. Through him go all stories transmitted by wire services such as the Associated Press, United Press International, Reuters, *The New York Times* and *The Los Angeles Times* and *The Washington Post* services and others. Before reaching the local telegraph editor, however, the stories pass other wire service editors who must put the stories on the wire from regional filing points. With science news, it appears that local telegraph editors exercise much control over the choice between a significant science news story and those which sound scientific, flashy and dramatic without having any close connection with new scientific developments.

Alton Blakeslee, the Associated Press science editor, once claimed he could make the front pages of every one of AP's more than 2,000 subscribers with a simple device. The trick was to mention in his opening paragraphs something about a treatment for piles, ulcers or sexual impotence. Every telegraph editor has these three conditions or worries about them, said Blakeslee (27).

So far as these personal concerns reflect those of larger segments within a listening, reading or viewing audience, however, they must be taken into consideration. This is what mass audience appeal is all about, in a sense. It undoubtedly helped a drug known as "L-Dopa" receive attention far out of proportion to the incidence of Parkinson's disease among mankind. (One unexpected effect of the drug: abnormal increase in sexual desire among a few patients.)

Science writers must convince their control centers of the merits of science news. One science writer received a note from her former city editor (located near San Francisco and Stanford University) saying that he had more confidence in the press releases put out by science-oriented businesses than in stories obtained by reporters from scientists (89).

Earl Ubell tells this story about a science writer he knows:

> Frequently the first time he writes a story it appears somewhere behind the financial pages in the newspaper. The second time he writes the same story, with approximately the same lead, it moves forward so that it might get on the second front page of the paper. And, finally, the third time around it almost always hits front page because by that time the editor has begun to understand that perhaps it is news and that he ought to do something about it [59:32].

John Troan, former NASW president, estimates that almost every adult American reader could be reached by science writers today except for the fierce competition for space and time. Readers are not interested in science alone, but also in politics, sports, business, labor, society news, neighborhood doings, accidents, crime, comics, crossword puzzles, novels and other features. He views editors as people who must be convinced readers want more news about more aspects of science than they now receive (258).

News of science or other topics means many things to many editors. Generally, says Professor John Hohenberg (99:63), the mass media observe three guidelines in selecting "news" from "non-news." The material must be new, defined broadly to include something the reader did not know yesterday. The material should be understood, of course, but also should not be misunderstood; therefore, the writer must explain how the material affects the reader, its importance and its significance. Accuracy must remain paramount at all times.

As Troan contends, the story stands little chance of being printed or read if it is not clear and interesting. Publication does not guarantee readership, although some stories have such direct effect that the reader will hunt for his information.

However, few science writers will disagree with Karl Abraham, science writer for *The Philadelphia Bulletin,* that the science news story or feature must stand on its own merit with other stories in competition for the space available (3). This means the reporter must first make his copy interesting and understandable to his own staff. Wilbourn McNutt, syndicated science writer, shows his stories to other members of the staff as a test of the reception they would receive at the control centers (152).

Summary

America and the world are caught up in an expansion of science and technology that cuts across all human endeavor. The social and economic effects have in many respects overrun the communications practices established in a more leisurely era. If the press, which includes all the communications media, discharges its obligation under the Constitution of the United States, it must abandon or modify the philosophies that built empires around reporting the interactions of men, women and guns. These may have been appropriately "newsy" in a more Victorian age when science was neither spectacular in itself nor a consumer of considerable public and private resources.

Dr. Polykarp Kusch, Nobel Prize winner in physics, offered this suggestion to a Pulitzer Prize jury:

> I think that science is frequently badly presented to the public. . . . The public is bombarded by news of ever-new triumphs of science and fails to understand that even science has its limitations. . . . A perceptive presentation by the press of the interdependence of science and society, the cultivation of the awareness that there is nothing that happens in our society that does not have roots in science—these are the things that the press must work at if it is to aid in the resolution of a crucial issue of the age, the attuning of man to a science-oriented world [131] .

Dr. Philip Abelson, president of the Carnegie Institution and editor of *Science,* sees a slightly different situation:

> It is true that the volume of news of science in daily newspapers is increasing. In Washington and New York, coverage is excellent; the writers are exceptionally competent, and sometimes adequate space is devoted to their stories. In other parts of the country science reporting ranges from fair to downright mediocre, or there is none at all.

> Some good, authoritative material is provided by the wire services, but local editors butcher it with a heavy hand. The material which is printed is usually gee-whiz, Buck Rogers distortions of the facts. Science writers for the wire services, wanting their copy to be used, tend to seek the more glamorous items. With distressing frequency scientist-operators are able to flim-flam the science writers with news stories which excite the imagination but have no solid technical basis. Local editors are especially susceptible to these worthless baubles, which they run in preference to less exciting items of solid merit [2:127] .

Thomas G. Fesperman, an executive of *The Charlotte Observer*, holds: "Every newspaper in the 25,000-and-up circulation brackets could use at least one reporter who is assigned to science" (74:45).

Victor K. McElheny, one of 16 on the Charlotte staff, parlayed his part-time science writing into a Nieman Fellowship with several years abroad as European correspondent for *Science* magazine and the post of science writer for *The Boston Globe.* Jean Gillette of the *San Angelo* (Texas) *Standard-Times,* a paper too small for much specialization, is a recent winner of the national science writing prize given yearly by the American Association for the Advancement of Science. Neither found their locale or their newspaper's size an impossible barrier to recognition of their skills as science writers.

John Lear, science editor of *Saturday Review,* finds most science writers too timid about tackling the large public questions with the same degree of critical evaluation, analysis and skepticism toward science and technology that journalists apply to other fields (137).

On the other hand, science writers have also shown the responsibility to pass up a sensational story and the toughness to battle scientists into a corner when the experts appear to overstate their findings. Scientists at a National Academy of Sciences press conference advised that women with a history of breast cancer should not nurse their babies. The scientists had found some mothers' milk contained particles resembling those from viruses known to transmit breast cancer in some strains of mice. The writers questioned the scientists until many uncertainties about the findings were established. The uncertainties included lack of proof of any connection between human mother's milk and breast cancer in daughters. Thus, a scare story was defused by the writers (137).

Finding the significance in science news is the science writer's most difficult task. Walter Sullivan of *The New York Times* believes that experience as a foreign correspondent or an investigative writer is useful training for spotting bias and seeking out other viewpoints. Scientists who personally seek publicity usually find their stories checked out more thoroughly than those which surface in the more conventional manner. Fear of presenting an unorthodox idea that may later prove unfounded should not inhibit the writer too greatly. Discovery and failure are part of the adventure of science. "There is joy, as well as wonder, in science, and the science writer should communicate as much of the joy as he can," says Sullivan (246).

In 1972, the Congress approved a $1.5 billion cure-oriented program against cancer. The relation of virus to human cancer had not yet been proved, but belief it would be found underlay almost all of the goals of the program. At least four cancer research institutions produced scientists who claimed to have found a "candidate virus" that would ultimately link a specific human virus to a particular type of cancer. So many virus discoveries were announced that writers saw a parallel between these and the spate of heart transplant operations that followed Dr. Christian Barnard's first effort in 1967.

These scientists short-circuited some of the scientific conventions by presenting their material at press conferences in advance of publication. Judith Randal of the *Washington Star* criticized both the scientists and their supervisors for the practice; she was also sharp with general reporters and television commentators who rushed the stories into circulation without drawing out how far the researchers were from actual proof of virus causation. "Quackery is quackery whether practiced by a witch-doctor or a Ph.D., and if glory-hungry scientists run wild, no matter how noble their motivation, the public stands to be the loser," she commented (194).

3
What Is
Science News?

What qualities lift a piece of research from a laboratory experiment into the realm of news? No simple definition can distinguish newsworthy stages of scientific endeavor, yet the scope of scientific development is so great that some boundaries must be staked out to guide one's writing about science.

Dr. Joel Hildebrand gave the following definition of one of the sciences, chemistry: "Chemistry is what chemists do and how they do it" (95:8).

A similar definition has been accepted by scientists working out a new science curriculum for elementary students:

> What is science? Is it the phyla of plants and classes of chemical reactions? Is it e = mc²? In other words, is it facts and theories about nature and experience? In part science is both of these, but perhaps even more, science is *what scientists do*, in short a process. . . . It is skills and attitudes which make the scientific enterprise so powerful. The belief is that the essence of science is its orderly, highly productive way of looking at nature and experience and squeezing from them their meaning [189].

Science is what scientists do. Writers can use this statement as a working motto. Any journalist who ignores the human element ignores vital information by omitting the role man plays in the process. As Dr. W.O. Baker, head of Bell Telephone Laboratories, pointed out:

> In truth, science is just old enough for us to know for sure that it is essentially a one-man job; that is, it can be done by one man at a time with help, of course, from students and disciples, and from the classic philosophies of all the other men and women that the scholar has always sought in fellowship. But technology, which is really the biggest part of what is called the Age of Science is also vastly more individualistic than we have admitted or even allowed up to now ... it offers the greatest chance man has yet had to express himself, to be each one of us a separate embodiment of the human spirit, to be truly personal [16:8].

Walter Karp, self-taught free-lance science writer, criticizes this "what scientists do" approach as being too limited. What we need, he maintains, is a new "language of natural philosophy." This should describe the qualities of science, the goals of scientists and the human, creative ways the search is conducted.

Creating this all encompassing "language of natural philosophy" will ease the understanding of science by the humanists. The burden, Karp believes, lies with the scientists because "only they know enough science" (122:16).

The writer who deals with a select population or occupation deals with people. The writer should know the less formalized activity of his people and recognize any potential story when he finds it. That alone argues for the writer specializing in science or any other special field to experience the broad apprenticeship of the generalist who knows a variety of stories.

The writer who regularly covers scientists stands the best chance of learning first what Lester Markel, former Sunday editor of *The New York Times,* calls "news": Information that is new, significant or dramatic (150).

A more specific definition of what writers and editors see as science news is contained in a questionnaire used by the National Association of Science Writers and the Survey Research Center of the University of Michigan:

It (science) includes everything scientists discover about nature—it could be the discoveries about the stars, or atoms, or about the human body or the mind—any basic discovery about how things work and why. But science also includes the way in which this information is used for practical uses—it might be a new way of curing a disease, or the invention of a new auto engine, or making a new fertilizer [127:3].

The survey directors used "science" as a general term covering pure and applied research for both medical and nonmedical activities as well as technology. The terms *science news* and *medical news* were used to separate events in physics, chemistry, astronomy, the social sciences and the like from items about medicine and public health.

Victor Cohn of *The Washington Post* describes his job this way:

Science, to the science reporter, is the man working in his laboratory. It is the search for truth—about people, about microbes, about atoms, about man. But science is more. If it were only a search for truth, there probably would not be many of us writing about it. It is also the search to know for man's use [53:750].

Categories of Science News

Science is a many-splintered thing; the multitude of categories scientists use to describe themselves run into the hundreds. Their work is underlaid by two main divisions: *pure* and *applied* research. These guide the science writer to understand the goal of each man's research. Is he searching for new knowledge? Is he attempting to solve a problem?

Scientists working toward one end may speak derisively of the others' goals. This is not the science writer's battle, however.

Sir George P. Thomson, master of Cambridge University's Corpus Christi College, believes both should be held in equal honor (255:996). He sees "pure science" as dealing in fundamentals as does religion and philosophy. Understanding the queer, apparently trivial details about the universe leads to a basic understanding of nature. "Applied science" aims at some amount of control over nature. Without technology, science is incomplete and inconclusive, he says. Medicine and commerce depend upon scientific fundamentals, and the desire to control nature keeps scientists close to reality.

National Science Foundation figures for one year show the relative economic positions for the divisions. Of nearly $16 billion in federal spending plans, 13 percent was designated for basic research. Applied research received about 21 percent, and the expensive business of developing actual hardware and engineering solutions to real problems in medicine, defense, space and transportation received 66 percent of the federal funds. This decade likely will see significant shifts in these allocations. The decline of defense and space expenditures brought the "development" share down from the high point of 79 percent (166). Inflation at the rate of more than 5 percent per year actually decreased the amount of R&D purchased.

Part of this shifting of funds will be the result of more emphasis in agencies where research and development programs were little known until recently. The research areas include ground transportation, crime and law enforcement, ecology, environment, pollution, waste disposal and the social sciences. Congress' demands to remove military funding from basic research, shifting the projects to off-campus or nonmilitary sponsorship, will change balances throughout the scientific and engineering communities.

The beginning science writer, be he a scientist or a journalist, should remember that scientific and engineering information is delivered on several levels. Between the elementary and the highly technical levels, he will find all shades of popularization.

Journals of the learned and professional societies publish reports, articles and papers in highly technical languages. These publications contain the discoveries and developments that interest the members of the organization. Acceptance for publication gives prestige to the author. It means that a board of his peers accepted it as meriting examination by the entire fraternity. The results and the procedures of the experiments are treated exhaustively so that other scientists may test the author's theories and results or use them in their own investigations.

Popular writers read these scientific journals for the seeds of a general interest science story which can be translated into less technical terms.

The nature of scientific research today makes these journal reports part of the public affairs reporting problem since most of the research is financed by federal grants.

There are two handicaps in relying upon these journals alone. Delays of weeks and months, await manuscripts submitted even when accepted; not all acceptable research gets published. Also, the proprietary interests in industrial research may cause a report to be withheld for a long time. The information may be new to the general reader and to the scientists of another discipline, but the writer's enthusiasm may be chilled by the knowledge that some professionals have known generally about the research for some time.

A second handicap in depending solely upon journals also relates to timeliness. Inevitably the writer will attend a press conference, a meeting of a scientific or engineering society or a speech where new material appears without the screening and analysis of an editorial board. This challenges the writer's knowledge, background and interrogatory techniques to evaluate the "newsiness" of the information and its importance. The author faced this problem unexpectedly when Dr. Albert Szent-Gyorgyi, revered Nobel laureate, suddenly released "admittedly incomplete research" (250:7) on two, almost identical natural chemicals found to promote and retard cancer growth by controlling cell growth. He said that all tissue seemed to contain "promine" and "retine" in nearly perfect balance. Recognition of the apparent proof of balance of naturally occurring compounds and of the respected performance of the scientist over several decades came from the writer's own background of reading and study. Even then he used the story only after double-checking with a biologist-physician who could analyze the newness and importance of the idea (38:1). Writers are extremely wary of all new drug claims.

Says Arthur J. Snider of *The Chicago Daily News:*

My concern is that the record would show that 90 per cent of the stories we have written about new drugs have gone down the drain as failures. We have either been deliberately led down the primrose path or have allowed ourselves through our lack of sufficient information to be led down the primrose path. The remaining 10 per cent of the drug stories we've written have had to be subjected to reevaluation. I think our mistakes arise from the fact that we are lacking knowledge on some factors in the experiment. . . . We may not know enough about curbing the built-in enthusiasm that an investigator may develop in his work [59:71].

Another level of technical information appears in the trade journals which are not as esoteric and difficult to understand as society journals. Because trade journal editors adopt a business viewpoint, information's news value depends greatly upon how soon this information can be adapted commercially.

Why Science News Should Be Reported

Several reasons have been reviewed for reporting news events in science. These reasons include the economic importance of science as an activity and of the products of scientific research. Interest exists for those already in scientific activity and those who will join some form of scientific endeavor as they grow old enough.

In a democracy, the growth of science in government demands reporting. The potential of scientific methods and brainpower does not escape those governments which are not always aligned with the Western world. A survey of 150 scientists from 30 countries indicated a belief that Russia attempts to utilize this pool of talent more than the United States (205:2).

Another argument for more science coverage by the mass media holds that scientific understanding is a cultural necessity. Dr. Paul B. Sears of Yale University urges a "scientific literacy" (219:10). Sir Charles Snow fears "two cultures," a situation void of communication and understanding between persons bound by scientific disciplines and those withdrawing from science to follow humanist disciplines entirely (230:4-42). Dr. Alan T. Waterman, former director of the NSF, does not see this sharp division between the world of science and the world of letters. The public may not need to know all the scientific details, Dr. Waterman holds, but does need a better understanding of what science is attempting to do (215:39). The broad and balanced view of science is particularly needed, he notes, where the scientific results affect public activity.

Such undertakings as the IGY, the Indian Ocean Survey and the Antarctic agreements that keep national territorial claims out of the southern continent indicate that scientific achievements can override national boundaries. This is not always possible for practitioners of the humanities, paradoxical as it sounds. Failure to recognize this seems to be the greatest weakness of arguments by such humanists as Jacques Barzun (18) against the growing preoccupation with scientific activity.

Gerald Holton, professor of physics at Harvard, does not cast all the blame for "scientific illiteracy" upon those outside the sciences.

> Too many scientists have forgotten that especially at a time of rapid expansion of knowledge they have an extra obligation and opportunity with respect to the wider public, that some of the foremost research men, including Newton and Einstein, took great pains to write expositions on the essence of their discoveries in a form intended to be accessible to the nonscientist [100:1187].

Dr. Holton maintains that this neglect increases the atomization of loyalties among scholars, writers, scientists, engineers, teachers, lawyers, politicians and the physicians. "Only very rarely does the professional feel a sense of responsibility toward or of belonging to, a larger intellectual community."

Why Science News Should Be Popularized

The American Institute of Physics has begun an aggressive public relations program for presenting difficult scientific fields to the layman. The AIP sponsors several seminars annually for writers, publishes glossaries that explain physics terms and offers the press popularized accounts of important articles in the AIP journals. These guides answer the question: why bother to interpret science to the layman anyway?

1. *Importance*: science is part of the general cultural knowledge as are art, literature, and drama.
2. *Political*: considerations for funds at national, state, and city levels for research and applications make it necessary that voters understand what is to be done by whom, and the possibilities and limitations as a basis for decision.
3. *Financial*: the ultimate financial support rests on laymen in public and private funding.
4. *Suspicion*: direct responsibility rests on science to show what it is doing in a direct and explicit way if it is to dispel anti-intellectual attitudes about this work.
5. *Compatibility*: the aims of scientists and journalists are compatible on the points of accuracy, and accuracy need not be sacrificed for interest.
6. *Bridging two worlds*: scientists must show their own desires to bridge any gap in understanding between the arts and sciences [125:4].

Science in a democracy may expect many people to comment on its practice and practitioners. For example, the Rev. James Keller writes:

Because you are a paying customer in man's space venture, make sure that everything done in the name of science is both an advance for humanity and an investment well made . . . Do what you can to make sure that science helps man and never harms him [124:17].

Ironically, scientific societies themselves are now rent by debating the purpose of scientific research in almost exactly these moral or ethical terms. Annual meetings of the American Association for the Advancement of Science, of the American Physical Society and of the American Sociological Association—to cite a few—have been thrown into turmoil by violent, noisy and extemporaneous clashes over science and the responsibilities of its practitioners. For every scientist who says his reponsibility ends with discovery of knowledge, there is another who says this responsibility extends the applications made of his discovery.

Without some public understanding of science, the ground rules established may be detrimental to the general body of scientists. The scientist cannot afford the short-sighted luxury of assuming that this may be a fault in the democratic institutions. Less democratic countries have made no pretense of allowing complete freedom of inquiry, even in the natural sciences. For example, historian David Joravsky of Brown University credits the political influence of agronomist Trofim D. Lysenko with keeping Russian biologists out of the mainstream of biological research in agriculture, genetics and heredity for 30 years (116).

Of "The Lysenko Affair" Dr. Joravsky noted: "To make a precise assessment of this, the indirect influence of ideology on Soviet biology, would be tantamount to writing a complete history of the U.S.S.R."

Historic and modern precedents exist for popularizing science. It was at a public lecture in 1847 that James Prescott Joule first announced his thesis that where force is destroyed by percussion, energy is transformed into the equivalent of heat; the first published account of Joule's idea appeared in a Manchester, England, weekly newspaper (111). Isaac Asimov, distinguished researcher for the Boston University School of Medicine, regularly writes such paperback books as *The Genetic Code* (12) for audiences seeking elementary scientific understanding.

Individual scientists will continue to control the press coverage they allow or encourage on their own individual research projects. But the picture of scientist-journalist cooperation is changing noticeably among those scientists who depend on public funds. Many writers feel the cooperation improves steadily.

This is the opinion of Art Snider of *The Chicago Daily News* after struggling with the problem for many years.

> The majority of scientists has come to develop the feeling that the press is trying to do a conscientious job. If the scientists have not completely bought the idea of press cooperation, they are at least taking it home on approval [35].

What are the aims of someone who popularizes scientific exploration? In accepting the United Nations' Kalinga Prize for his popular science articles, author Jean Rostand said that popularization should introduce the greatest number of people to "that which is the glory of the human mind" and bring them closer to "the men who struggle against nature" (203). He made these points:

1. Popularization continues, corrects and fills gaps left in school education which lags behind progress.
2. Popularization arouses the desire to take up research and directly benefits creative science.
3. Popularization acquaints the public at large with the power and efficiency of creative science.
4. Popularization creates a link between specialists in different disciplines since it is popularization which ensures that the physicist is not altogether unaware of what is happening in biology or the reverse.
5. Popularization keeps, or could keep, politicians informed, and politicians have an ever greater need to be familiar with scientific developments.

Predicting that the man-in-the-street will have an increasing amount to say about the social, national, moral and intellectual issues raised by applied science, Rostand declared:

> Science not only affects us at any given moment in our day-to-day existence, it dogs us, it pursues us. Have we not, all of us, been transformed

into involuntary guinea pigs ever since atomic fission, without asking our opinion, began to plant harmful particles in our bones? The obligation to endure gives us the right to know [203:1495].

One barrier to understanding and popularization is the language of science. This specialized language of precise technical terms laced with jargon is not spoken by the layman. Often scientists in one field cannot understand the language of another. Yet, some scientists object to "popularizing" on the grounds that subjects cannot be clearly discussed outside the "language of science." But there is not one language of science but several.

Edward G. Boring of Harvard University has chided his colleagues who believe they should not depart from the "language of science." In a letter to *Science* (33:610), Dr Boring said:

1. Scientists do not talk "that way" all the time, even with students.
2. Scientists do not talk "that way" with their wives.

"For myself, I take the use of the scientific language more lightly, less rigorously, and I am glad that most of my colleagues do too," he said.

Dr. Sidney Farber, professor of pathology at Harvard's Medical School, once said:

I'd like to digress a moment and speak of a lesson I learned when I was very young from someone very close to me who was not medically or scientifically trained at all. What she said was that if I could not present a paper or write a paper in language understandable to her in all likelihood the material was not understandable to me either [59:12].

John Troan, former president of the National Association of Science Writers, maintains (258:1193) the surest way to prevent the understanding of science is to interpret it as though it were a secret ritual practiced only by the ordained. It is to the scientists' own interest to take a hand in the public education in science.

Dr. Joel H. Hildebrand was not adverse to revealing a human, often illogical, picture of the scientist at work:

I distinguish two aspects of science; one may be designated *content* the other, *enterprise.* The one is, as the dictionary says, classified knowledge; the other is the ways in which scientists work and think. The one is the way we write up our results, in papers and books, in the passive voice, giving the impression that we start with precise measurements and proceed by strict logical steps to incontrovertible conclusions. The other is the way we really do it–starting with hunches, making guesses (most of which prove to be wild), making many mistakes, going off on blind roads before hitting on one that seems to be going in the right direction. That is science in the making [95:7].

The American Association for the Advancement of Science is the largest of all scientific societies. Its Committee on Science in the Promotion of Human Welfare has recommended four goals for improving public understanding.

1. Stimulation of discussion, within the scientific community, of issues relating sciences and human welfare.
2. Assembly of facts relevant to a given issue via *ad hoc* committees, conferences, and etc. for dissemination to the scientific community.
3. Preparation and dissemination of reports for the general public, translations for distribution to the public media.
4. Development of liaison between scientists and the public on a local basis through local civic groups [198:68].

Doctors, for reasons to be discussed later, remain something of a problem. However, Dr. John E. Allen points out (199:75) that doctors are not as "scared" of reporters as they were 20 years ago. Many doctors, showing a change of attitude, welcome publicity. This improved cooperation must be a two-way street, however, said the editor of the *American Medical Association News* (197:55) in criticizing medical reporting on two points: blowing a medical story up beyond its proportion in the eyes of the profession and premature disclosure of promising results. Both raise too many false hopes.

These criticisms appear somewhat justified in other fields of research also. Within this context, it is easy to see why many science reporters prefer to depend upon publication of a paper or the delivery of a report to constitute the "news break." Such criticisms will occur again as they have in the past; no system— including science—achieves perfection.

Earl Ubell, while writing on *The New York Herald Tribune,* remembered when cancer researchers first heard someone stand up in a meeting and propose that viruses might cause leukemia in mice normally resistant to leukemia.

> As a result of this, the poor man was nearly flayed alive by the kind of people who would have disauthenticated his report and would have told us not to write about it, and did tell us not to write about it. Nevertheless, just last year [1962] he won a UN prize of $10,000 for this discovery [59:36].

And 10 years later, cancer researchers were still trying to pin down the virus responsible for even one form of human cancer.

Error is also a two-way street. Ultimately the writer's responsibility rests upon individual responsibility.

"Discovery" or "Process"

The beginning science writer should remain conscious of a deep disagreement about "What is science news?" Both the scientists and the writers are divided on this question. It lies at the heart of the conflict between writers and those scientists who fear "overemphasis" and "prematurity." It lurks behind the discontent many science writers feel with their daily reporting task. It involves the writers' and the scientists' understanding of background, perspective, significance and accuracy. The disagreement over "What is science news?" operates significantly in writing about science and public affairs.

Is science news a series of events, new scientific findings, the discoveries made by scientists?

Or is science news the way in which science and medicine move forward across a wide front, grasping new understanding of their broad themes?

One is the story of a single man or a group of men. The other is the story of many men in many places.

Dennis Flanagan, former science writer for a weekly magazine and now editor of *Scientific American*, etched this conflict very sharply:

> The fact remains that the ruling concept of news is the concept held by the daily newspaperman. News is something that happens on a particular day: a political event, say, or an ax murder.

> This concept is reasonable in its place, but it plays hob with the journalism of science and medicine. Scientific progress is not packaged obviously in daily events in spite of such artificial newspegs as the publication of a paper or presentation at a scientific meeting. . . . Nevertheless, the ruling definition of news is the event.

> This concept of news interacts disastrously with the concept of the scientific finding. . . . The journalist of science can only operate by thinking in terms of broad themes, and yet he is obliged to cut up these themes into little pieces to fit the canon of news . . . .

> The marriage of the news story and the scientific finding gives both of them a curiously ghostly quality. At best it substitutes an occasional tree for the forest. How many new drugs, how many new surgical procedures have we read about and forgotten because we did not know how they fitted in with the broad picture of medicine? . . . Science and medicine are much more than an endless procession of findings. . . . I take it as an article of faith that the aspiration of the journalist of science and medicine is to explain to his fellow laymen what science and medicine are. . . . It would be much better if the journalist used his knowledge of the important themes in science to convey the theme itself, not its disconnected parts. . . .

> But if the journalist of science and medicine does not write stories about findings, what does he write? An example that comes easily to mind . . . was a well-rounded account of where surgery stands today in terms of one of its leading practitioners and innovators. I also observe

with interest that when *The New York Times* prints an account of an important scientific finding these days the account is often accompanied by a separate box on the character of the man who made the finding. . . . One wants to know what kind of a fellow a scientist is, what made him decide to do what he is doing, and what he thinks that he and his peers are learning.

Many well-meaning people seem to regard science and medicine as being closed theological systems that do not permit any disagreement. . . . It seems to me that the reporting of mere findings contributes to this misconception. To many, such accounts represent the establishment loftily handing down the truth according to its dogma. Such a view could not survive if those who hold it could see science and medicine as a collection of individuals rather like themselves, seeking knowledge but never cocksure about it, and trying to enlarge it by resourcefully applying the limited means at their disposal . . . [59:14-16].

A critical aspect of this approach was spotlighted by Dr. James Shannon, former director of the National Institutes of Health:

But it presents a new set of problems to the science reporter. . . . Stories of that general sort are necessarily interpretive in nature, since science is outside the day-to-day experience of the reader. The writing must be interpretive and highly editorialized. . . . A good deal of our trouble comes from that—the editorialization of the fact, rather than the fact itself. In order to explain the advance, it often becomes necessary to discuss the mechanics by which it took place, the investigator as a person, and the relationship of the advance to the generalities of science both in retrospect and prospect. That may be a tall order, but nonetheless these are the essentials of a good interpretive story of scientific progress. . . .

In my experience, most bad reporting comes either from a frivolous disregard for the serious matter that is being reported or from the fact that the man who writes the story can't get it published unless he finds some peg to hang it on. It's usually the newspeg that causes the distorted headline and the rewrite job that really does damage to science.

I'd like to comment specifically in relation to the problem of context. I think it's quite beyond expectation to find any news items that relate to science (and in general they're five or six inches in one of the middle pages of the newspaper) the context of the discovery described in any depth. On the other hand, the discovery or advance can be presented as a step in a series of advances that have gone before and will continue. This context can be covered in a few lines without going into detail of the total background [59:40].

Earl Ubell writes both "discovery" and "process" stories about science, as do most science writers. A process of correction through repetition operates in the daily press, in his view.

What one can say, then, about contextual material in the public press (that is, the the mass media) is this: that we cannot transmit this evolutionary concept that you're talking about too well in a short period of time; that what we have to do is act as an alerting mechanism, and those who wish to get more and deeper information on which to act or to incorporate into their own intellectual ideas probably will have to go to other sources of information. Over the long period of time, by the repetitive character of newspaper and magazine and television reporting, we probably will get information across. I would not, then, be too disturbed by the single hot item which appears from time to time. That's the newspaper and the magazine ringing a bell and saying, "Look; this is interesting and important." Perhaps you ought to look elsewhere for more information [59:40].

William P. Steven, of *The Chicago Daily News* and a booster of both the Council for the Advancement of Science Writing and the National Association of Science Writers, makes these related points:

As to the necessity of incorporating the full background in each science story, I think this is again an idealistic achievement. . . . Condensation is a great art, but there are points where it simply is impossible, where the

choice has to be made as to whether you carry the relatively brief report
or whether you carry nothing; and that choice has to be made simply out
of the economics of the newspaper business. . . . We've got to tell these
important stories many times. This matter of repeating is terribly important. . . . Occasionally, an editor will get enough insight into a series of
these little stories that we're all complaining about so that he grasps the
fact that there is some relationship and some continuity. Then it is
possible, if he has enough manpower and you can afford it, to take a man
and put him on a story of this kind and say, "Do me a Series" or "Do me
a major piece for Sunday." [59:41-42] . . . .

Who Reads Science News?

Science and medical news do not interest everyone. Hardly
anything in a newspaper or a magazine does. Yet three readership
studies—one very old (249) and two fairly new (130;154)—
indicate that these stories have a high and consistent reader interest. The changes in this interest over more than 20 years are significant because the factors creating it are operating today in increasing strength.

Eric Ashby, master of Cambridge University's Clare College,
stated some handicaps to popularizing science in an article entitled
"Dons or Crooners?" for *Science* (11:68-70). As viewed by Sir
Eric:

1. Generally science will not help most people earn more
   money or be more useful around the house.
2. Busy men and women at the end of a working day are
   tired and admittedly deserving of some relaxation.
3. Science as a subject is highly professionalized even for
   extraordinarily intelligent laymen.
4. Ultimately there is the question of why scientists should
   compete with crooners.

An identifiable demand for science and medical news existed
before the opening of the space age in 1957. Perhaps it is too
strong to label as a "demand." It is doubtful that readers will

organize protests if this news was omitted as they do when comic strips or sports pages are left out. Newspaper readers are better compared with sponges, with a considerable number willing to soak up news of new developments in science and medicine.

One of the earliest readership studies covered 130 newspapers from 1939 to 1950 (249:411-15). News of science and invention, health and safety ranked twelfth. This was behind the comic strips, war, defense, fire and disaster, human interest, weather, major crime news, "events of significance to society as a whole," consumer information and certain unclassifiable items.

Lest this sound too discouraging, these stories of science-medicine ranked higher than sports, art, music, literature, accidents, national government, local government and recreation.

The study showed that interest in these pre-Sputnik years remained at a respectable 20 percent of total readership. Assuming 300,000 subscribers for a successful metropolitan newspaper, science in these years commanded about 60,000 readers.

Two later readership studies were commissioned by the National Association of Science Writers. Both were conducted by the Survey Research Center at the University of Michigan. Both studies are now out of print but may be found in many libraries and schools of journalism. *Science, the News and the Public* (130:1-43) resulted from a 1957 survey made before the first Sputnik. *Satellites, Science, and the Public* (148) resulted from another survey that following the launching of the first satellites.

From them, Dr. Hillier Krieghbaum, chairman of the NASW surveys committee and an associate professor of journalism at New York University, has drawn most of the material about science readership cited in current literature. The "science reader," says Dr. Krieghbaum (130:4), is a middle-aged high school graduate. He lives in the West or Middle West, usually in a community of 2,500 to 50,000 of in metropolitan suburbs. He belongs to several organizations, reads two newspapers daily, takes two or three magazines, listens to the radio for an hour and watches television longer. He is well-informed in national politics and foreign events. He leans on his newspaper and magazines for intellectual content.

Before Sputnik, the surveys showed, less than 50 percent of the adult population was aware of the idea of man-made satellites. After Sputnik, 90 percent of the people interviewed were aware of the satellites. Author of the post-Sputnik study concluded (154:50) that awareness of a scientific event may be stimulated by news of the event if it's available and public reaction is largely motivated by a desire to understand and master the world as seen by the individual.

> Another point that stands out is that a sizable group of individuals are curious about anything in science. That is true even when it concerns such topics as molecular structure and stellar discovery. Some editors and publishers would dismiss both these as too abstract and non-practical for much coverage, but they would attract one reader out of every seven [130:21].

Wilbur Schramm of the Institute for Communication Research at Stanford University analyzed most of the readership studies for the American Association for the Advancement of Science. The analysis considered what people know about science, where they get their information, what they understand about science and technology and their impression of the scientists. In *Science and the Public Mind* (210), Dr. Schramm extracted these 12 tenets useful for science writers:

1. Knowledge of science is widely, but not deeply, distributed in the United States; there are still large areas of ignorance.
2. An individual's education is the chief predictor of his science knowledge.
3. Mass media use is the second predictor of scientific information; after the school years, most of the increment of science knowledge comes from the media.
4. Where one goes for scientific information depends on the topic and one's own characteristics. (Medical news is read mostly by women, other science news by men.) Seeking

professional advice is governed by the individual's interpretation of the seriousness of the problem or his need for knowledge.

5. The more personalized and/or sensationalized a scientific article is, the larger its audience.

6. The mass media tend to use these techniques in reporting science and to select material that can be so treated:

    a. If you can put something in story form, it will be read by more people.

    b. If you can make it apply to the reader, more will read it.

    c. If you can stress the sensational elements in it (the conflict or violence or unusualness) or the human interest elements, it will be read by more people.

    d. If you can personalize it, it will be more widely read; this refers both to personalizing the meaning of the story and personalizing the author.

7. The mass media do not apply to entertainment material the same standards of scientific accuracy that they apply to advice and reportorial descriptions. (On mental health, for instance, the views presented in plays, serials, stories, comics and so forth are apt to be presented in the most stereotyped and outdated way. By contrast, however, scientific material in comic panels devoted to science is most likely to aim at presenting the newest material possible.)

8. Public attitudes toward science and scientists are generally favorable, although not very accurately informed.

9. The public is interested in getting more scientific information.

10. There are some negative indicators as to what information on science should be given the public. (Some new information creates such anxiety that readers will reject it; there is a point beyond which the arousal of fear or unease will result, not in more attention, but in rejection.)

11. Learning new scientific information does not necessarily set into motion a logical chain of belief attitude and behavior.
12. Some actions on the part of scientists are indicated.

Dr. Schramm recommended on the final point that the scientist pay closer attention to school curricula in science and to the level of science teaching, opening their doors to children who are the future scientists.

Specifically he suggested for the science writer that scientists contribute to educating the science writer and to making information about their work easier to get. Surveys of reader interest have not, to date, probed deeply into the science information consumed by very young readers. However, the increased emphasis on science courses in the junior high schools and high schools seems to indicate an increased interest through "scientific literacy." In Houston, for example, 71 youths, 14 to 18, organized a Boy Scouts of America Explorer Troop to develop their knowledge of science.

Dr. Percy H. Tannenbaum, director of the Mass Communications Research Center at the University of Wisconsin, does not quite accept the idea of writing science news for the masses. He told NASW members that his studies suggest science news "is another such specialized communications situation" as sports or business. Writers, according to Dr. Tannenbaum, not only waste their time translating science news into laymen's language but also risk alienating "science-readers" without gaining any "nonreaders." Dr. Tannenbaum fears that too much popularization will drive away scientists and "the self-selected part of the audience most interested in science news *qua* science news" (172:6).

What will be the reaction to pumping more life and dramatic detail (sensationalizing) into science news stories? Earl Ubell, who has tried it in his newspaper, says the effect is good.

Perhaps one could "jazz it up." So we performed an experiment in our survey. . . . In general, the jazzed up version attracted more interest than did the straightforward presentation. Some of us felt that this mild sensationalism would not be worthwhile if in the process we lost our more sophisticated readers. Interestingly enough, the better-educated individuals were almost as susceptible to this approach as were the people who were barely interested in science [263].

So, you can entertain without sacrificing readership. Samuel Lubell, one of the most vigorous pollsters of public opinion, believes the masses of people probably can master complicated detail as well as the more educated (145:1-30).

I have done surveys of attitudes on automobiles and lawn-growing and have been astonished at the amount of complex, technical information the average man possessed *on things that interest him.*

The public also draws a tremendous amount of scientific information from television programs aimed primarily at entertainment, says E.G. Sherburne, who directed studies in the public understanding of science for the American Association for the Advancement of Science. Writing in *Journalism Quarterly* (221:305), he suggests that there may be as much drama in the radiation laboratory as in the city hospital. There are the same tense moments, the joys of success and discovery, the despairing moments, the struggles and the challenges.

In the same issue of *Journalism Quarterly* devoting a special section to science reporting, Kenneth G. Johnson (113:315-322) found newspaper editors using different yardsticks to judge science stories than the readers, the scientists and the science writers. Editors stressed "color" and "excitement" first in rating the value of a science story. "Accuracy" and "significance" were secondary. Readers, science writers and scientists placed first importance on "accuracy" and "significance."

Reminiscent of a popular beer commercial, editors preferred science stories "exciting, colorful, clear, and light." "Only the editor group stands apart," Dr. Johnson concluded.

> In terms of both dimension of judgment and specific judgment, the science writers appear to be better mediators than the editors. Their dimensions of judgment are essentially those used by scientists, readers, and non-readers [112:322].

Dr. Joshua Lederberg of Stanford University, with some understanding of newspaper operations, has made two suggestions for improving science-medical reporting. One was that copy desks make fewer changes in stories for the benefit of headlines and sensational approach. His other suggestion was to do away with the idea that science writers have to meet sharp deadline pressures. "Science writers who are well-trained can write splendid feature articles and columns. The news items written under pressure are generally hack jobs" (81:9).

Russian Science Writing

Popular science writing in Russia presents a checkered picture. Any assessment of the quality there depends upon your viewpoint and the material examined.

Jonathan Leonard, in *Time*, cites examples of science writing that outdo science fiction. Science writers Genrikh Saulovich Altov and Valentian Nikolaevna Zhuravlyova attributed a string of craters in Siberia to the effects of a powerful laser beam fired from a planet circling the star 61 Cygni. The distance: 66 trillion miles from Earth. Leonard said the Russians reported that when Krakatoa erupted in 1883 it generated many radio waves which reached 61 Cygni about 11 years later. In the view published by the Russians, the Cygnian scientists took this as a message from Earth scientists. Cygnians blasted the craters while attempting to send a reply over a laser beam. Observed *Time:*

Russia's romantic science reporters have never been willing to settle for the most likely explanation—that the big blast was caused by an outsized meteorite. Some of them insist that it was caused by a comet; others prefer to believe that a huge extraterrestrial spaceship crashed in Siberia, or perhaps jettisoned nuclear fuel that exploded and dug the crater [139:49].

A group of students from Tomsk University reported unusual radioactivity still existing in the crater in 1959. So many Russians accepted this that the Soviet Academy of Sciences sent in a team of investigators; the scientists found no radioactivity above that of the natural background.

Russian science writing, says Leonard, is filled with accounts of abominable snowmen, salamanders that return to life after being frozen 5,000 years, devices that yield more energy than is put into them, monsters that leave tracks on the ocean bottom, ice that does not melt and other mysterious events.

Official Soviet science writing, by contrast, seems competent but dull. Even propaganda against the "capitalists" was muted in several stires from the APN *Newsletter of Science and Engineering* (10:1-15). The weekly newsletter is published in Russian, English, French, German and Spanish. It is distributed through the official Novosti Press Agency in Pushkin Square, Moscow.

Bryant Kearl, professor of agricultural journalism at the University of Wisconsin, reports that the Soviets held their first American-style science writing seminar in the fall of 1962. This, said Kearl, marked the beginning of science popularization as official policy. A hundred members of the All-Union Forum of Journalists attended the eight-day meeting in Moscow. *Pravda* began a regular section called "In the World of Science." The seminar recommended that journalists reporting science and technology organize into an independent branch of the Creative Commission of the U.S.S.R. Union of Journalists. They were warned against being superficial in covering the science news and admonished to avoid insisting that all articles be put into "some kind of newspaper language," said Kearl (123:1). The Soviet writers were advised to concentrate on applied science and technology.

Japan's Science Writers

In the fall of 1963, the author had the pleasure of entertaining three Japanese newsmen touring U.S. science and space establishments. The team's leader, Takuji Makino of the *Yomiuri Shimbun*, discussed several aspects of science writing in Japan that differ from practices in this country (146).

Japanese science writers are chosen with consideration for their training in scientific, engineering and technical areas. The large number of graduates from Japanese universities and the general hiring practices of the Japanese newspapers provide time to teach beginners how to write science news. Because of so much manpower and because Japanese newspapers are small in comparison to U.S. newspapers, beginners may practice for more than a year before any of their efforts reach print. The reporters and writers are organized in a paramilitary fashion under "captains" such as Makino.

Akio Akagi, a producer of science programs for the Japan Broadcasting Corporation, compiled a more statistical summary of Japanese science writing (6:3). The mass media in Japan have more than 300 science specialists, he reported. Their increase after Sputnik in 1957 was accelerated by a 1960 report from the National Committee of Science and Technology which recommended public enlightenment as part of a 10-year plan to develop science and technology in Japan.

A common science writing technique of the Japanese adds a scientific explanation to the straight reporting. For example, an account of a nuclear explosion or a gas explosion will carry illustrated sidebars describing the blast's physical and chemical causes and the biological effects.

This technique has three advantages: it helps clarify what has happened, it holds interest better than would a science story not connected with a news event, and it promotes cooperation among science popularizers and journalists in other fields [6:3].

Similar use is made in the United States of science and medical specialists, as will be discussed later. One example is a story written by Harold M. Schmeck, Jr. of *The New York Times* News Service (209:13). When the Warren Commission report on the assassination of President John F. Kennedy was released, Schmeck was assigned the task of explaining the autopsy report and the extent of physical damage of each bullet.

Akagi emphasizes that much remains to be done in Japan to improve public knowledge of science. He reported that one survey showed that only 13.4 percent of a group of newspaper readers could fully comprehend science stories as presented (6:3). Compare this with the results of similar studies for American readers.

American science writers, it seems, have plenty of company in their desire to find out how to explain science to their subscribers and how to entice the reader into the story.

It is the writer, now, who must cultivate what Edward Edelson, science commentator for radio and the *New York Daily News,* calls "the essential talent that any science writer needs, the ability to digest an abstruse theory and excrete it in readable, understandable form" (70).

4
Writing
Science News

In 1964, representatives of 21 scientific societies joined writers, university officials, newspaper executives and government leaders at a testimonial dinner. The man they honored was stubby, grey-haired William L. Laurence, retiring science editor of *The New York Times*.

"Bill Laurence has probably done as much as any single man during a generation to further the public understanding of science," stated the announcement (126).

Few writers in any field expect the almost universal acceptance accorded Laurence during his 34 years of reporting. Making the honor even more distinctive, the tribute was given by scientists to one who was not a scientist. He smuggled himself out of Europe in a pickle barrel, studied liberal arts at Harvard and spent most of his life as a newspaperman. His newspaper colleagues awarded him a share of the 1937 Pulitzer Prize. In 1946 his stories about the development of nuclear fission and the atomic bomb in World War II won him another Pulitzer Prize. With lesser brilliance, most science writers have followed the professional path blazed by Laurence.

Education for Science Writing

Wherever writers, editors and scientists gather, a continuing debate is over the best way to prepare for a science writing career. Certainly the education and backgrounds of those who write most of today's science news provides little basis for judgment.

For most members of the science press, it merely "happened" that assignment by assignment they grew to spend most of their time writing about science. An informal poll of 30 science writers covering a large scientific meeting turned up only one trained in science. Earl Ubell, holder of a B.S. in physics, now has more science-trained associates. The predominant tone remains journalistic. Dr. Irving S. Bengelsdorf, former science editor of *The Los Angeles Times*, earned his science doctorate and worked as a scientist and industrial executive before turning to prize-winning science journalism. H. Jack Geiger, M.D., left international News Service as a science writer; after earning his medical degree, he pioneered, in Mississippi and Boston, the delivery of new types of medical care to the urban and rural poor. While practicing science writing, Blair Justice of *The Houston Post* took his doctorate in psychology, and in the fire of the "long hot summers" of urban riots became a part-time and later a full-time advisor to his city's government. In his writings, he communicates as a professional social scientist, as an essential member of the local government and as a journalist using the best scientific knowledge to explain to laymen the changes around them.

Performance in print determines who is a "good" science writer. The question of "what" makes a good science writer finds less general agreement among the science writers than "who" writes the best science stories. Throughout this study, the literature has carried a running discussion, wry and half-humorous, about the need for organizing science education for the journalist. However, it was not until the fall of 1964 that the question seemed to move toward some degree of polarization.

Dr. James Stokley, chairman of the professional training committee of the NASW, touched it off with his formal committee report (235). Dr. Stokley occupies a unique position in science

writing. Simultaneously he holds associate professorships in journalism and in physics and astronomy at Michigan State University.
He teaches science and journalism and writes technical and popu
lar science articles. Professor Stokley's committee report, printed
in the September, 1964, issue of the *NASW Newsletter,* proposed
an education program heavily oriented toward science courses.

In the same issue, on the editorial page, a vigorous objection
was written by the editor and former NASW president:

> No one, at this point, knows what background is required to make a
> good science writer. This is one of the unknowns that should be ascer-
> tained. We can only hope that what we like to call our off-spring organi-
> zation, the Council for the Advancement of Science Writing, can find out
> for us. . . . We do not believe the [Stokley] committee has scientific data
> to back its conclusions. To let this go unchallenged might create the false
> impression that the committee opinions are accepted as NASW doctrine.
> The Executive Committee . . . was not in agreement with the report. We
> feel that the majority of NASW members hold dissentient opinions
> [93:40]. . . .

The year 1963-64 also marked the beginning of a training
program sponsored by the council for the Advancement of Science
Writing. The differences between the Stokley approach and the
CASW plan are so vast as to merit detailed examination.

The Stokley Approach

Genesis of the Stokley report is seen in a statistical survey of
72 science writers. William E. Small, studying for an M.A. degree
under Dr. Stokley, made the survey and published the results in
the *NASW Newsletter* of December, 1963.

> Results of the survey seem to support a program especially designed for a
> science writer—emphasis on English and journalism, balanced with several

survey courses in the sciences and concentration on one or two selected sciences. They also point out the need for at least four years of college, perhaps as much as a master's degree. And they suggest that on-the-job training should coincide with or follow formal college education [225:12].

Small found the average science writer had spent 24 years in professional writing with 14 in science writing. Thirty-eight percent said a bachelor's degree was desirable in a science writer; 18 percent would add a master's, and 28 percent said that training should include "as much as possible" formal education.

The respondents to Small's questionnaire gave several areas of competence. The top seven areas, in descending order, were medicine, biology, psychology, chemistry, astronomy, physics and space technology. In the same order the writers most frequently covered medicine, biology, physics, psychology, astronomy, space technology and chemistry. The writers had the most formal training in mathematics, about 2.9 semesters. Following came biology, chemistry, physics, psychology, medicine and geography. When asked to recommend courses for a science-writing student, writers listed English most often. Next came biology, chemistry, physics, mathematics, history and reporting. The writers said they found field reporting most important for their own training. Then came science courses, scientists, science seminars, newspapers, science-writers seminars, their colleagues and scientific conventions. They ranked editors last (225:14).

Nine months later Professor Stokley proposed a fairly definite educational program. He acknowledged that several of the best science writers had little or no formal science training but drew upon their reading, study and contacts with scientists. The increasing complexity of science makes it more difficult for journalists to acquire the broad knowledge needed by private study alone, he said (235:19). He recommended a bachelor's degree with a major in one science or in a broader area such as the physical or biological sciences.

The CASW Approach

Pierre C. Fraley, then executive secretary of the Council for the Advancement of Science Writing (CASW), inaugurated a vastly different program in 1963 to give 60 to 70 general assignment reporters on-the-job training.

In describing the program, Fraley said (77:2) one of the quickest and most effective ways of developing skill and facility was to cover large national or scientific or medical meetings beside experienced science writers. Two such meetings were required for trainees in the year's work. At each an experienced writer served as writer-in-residence to deliver a series of seminars on science writing and to act as counselor.

Trainees received subscriptions to seven periodicals including *Medical World News, Physics Today, Science* and *Scientific American*. They were given five books for reference and background: *A Short History of Science* by William C. Dampier; *Science and Human Values* by J. Bronowski; *The Scientific American Reader,* an anthology; *What Is Science,* edited by J.R. Newman; and *An Intelligent Man's Guide to Science* (two volumes) by Isaac Asimov.

The trainees also received a chapter from *Goals for Americans,* Warren Weaver's "The Great Age of Science." Reference works included the pocketbook *Guide to Science Reading,* a bibliography compiled by Hilary Deason; 15 glossaries of physics terms from the American Institute of Physics; a glossary on psychology; *Merck Index,* a standard medical reference; *Merck Veterinary Manual; Stedman's Medical Dictionary*; and the *Concise Dictionary of Science,* Frank Gaynor editor.

CASW put this project on a more local basis in 1965. Trainees, and their trainers, were recruited on a state wide basis and urged to concentrate on state and regional science news.

Fraley held that while the term "science writer" should be interpreted broadly, the professional scientist likely will not make an adequate newspaper or magazine science writer (80).

Scientists have excelled as writers of popular books about science, said Fraley, but only occasionally as writers of magazine articles. Few have written directly for newspapers.

To zero in on this issue: Should it be the scientist who reports—primarily through the newspapers—the day-to-day events and occurrences in the world of science? It is my feeling that very few scientists are either equipped to do this or have the inclination or the time to do it conscientiously on a continuing basis. Also there is a fallacy that having detailed, technical knowledge about a subject automatically confers an ability to communicate and be articulate about it [80:23].

The program continues today, guided by Henry A. Goodman, the present CASW secretary.

In the years following the launching of Russia's Sputnik, many programs were launched to give a type of first-aid training to journalists. Under Prof. John Foster at Columbia University, fellowships provided by the Sloan and Rockefeller foundations allowed more than 100 journalists and scientists to follow individualized programs aimed at increasing the number of skilled communicators in science, engineering, medicine and technology. The Nieman fellowship program at Harvard always has one grant reserved for a science writer. The effect of these programs has been to spread the number of full- or part-time science writers more broadly across the communications establishment. As a consequence, the training of science communicators has been integrated into many schools of journalism and departments of science and engineering.

It may be that the writer seeks his own professional level, improving his skills against new challenges. The freedom of movement within the communications field attracts many different people. If you explore the broader philosophical relationships of science and journalists, and their mutual futures, *Science and the Mass Media* by Hillier Krieghbaum (New York University: 1967) offers valuable insights.

As suggested in *Journalism Quarterly* by J. Ben Lieberman and Penn T. Kimball (143 527-34), professors at the Columbia journalism school, it may be a hopeless task to train writers for a seemingly endless line of specialties. The ability to locate specialized material, visualize it, communicate it and contribute perspective to an event may be the guiding factors, as they visualize them, favoring a generalist approach.

The valleys and peaks in the educational attention given to science during the past twenty-five years, for example, have had myriad effects not only on scientific progress, but also on the money and effort available to other crucial areas of learning. As attention focused upon science, non-scientific specialities sometimes lost ground. As the supply and demand for talents shift among various specialties, flexibility and occupational mobility are important elements in a free system [143:529].

The science writers themselves do not say that only "science specialists" should portray science for the public. Commented Walter Sullivan of *The New York Time*:

We cannot permit this job to be done only by the science writers, that the telling of the story of science and its social, economic, and political ramifications also involves the general reporter and editor. He needs an awareness for this, because science is so basic a part of the story today, and if we expect the public to become aware of this, certainly the average general newspaper reporter and editor must take part in this too [59:74].

Science writers arrive at their jobs many ways. Some are appointed from the pool of reporters and copy editors. Ralph O'Leary, the late science editor and city editor of *The Houston Post,* once observed that the writer who could master the detail of courthouse reporting likely could become a competent science writer (175:1).

William P. Steven says he seeks proof of applicants' ability to communicate in scientific matters by studying their scores on scientific testing scales and by reviewing their grades in science courses at college (233).

Many ways exist for a person to fill gaps in his education when he decides that his interests lead him to science writing. Formal academic training may suit those with the time and opportunity. Auditing courses in science, attending public lectures and sitting in scientific conventions are inexpensive methods for the writer who feels he lacks the technical competence for course credit.

Geologist William J. Cromie started writing during the long nights he spent on a floating ice island, a scientific station in the Arctic. He now heads a science news service.

Science writers must conduct an outside reading program. No one can expect to know all fields of science, but a general knowledge of most fields is required on a science beat. Science writers are not specialists in a narrow sense of the word. In one week a writer may interview a biologist, cover a medical meeting, discuss both policy and technical developments in the space program, turn out a piece on astronomy, attend a physicist's press conference, research an article on atomic energy and perhaps explain the meteorological aspects of a heat wave or a cold snap.

Many books will come to the writer from various publishing houses. Inexpensive paperback books have simplified access to broad areas of science. The Mentor Books (New York: New America Library) and the Doubleday Science Study Series (Garden City, New York: Anchor Books, Doubleday and Company, Inc.) have helped the author. Familiarity with popular books establishes an understanding of many fields and a level of science writing and analogy that fits a mass audience. It is worth remembering at this point that while a reader may have received his doctorate in physics, he may well have had his last biology course in high school or as a college freshman.

Required reading for beginning and veteran science writers include a number of professional journals and weekly or monthly magazines. *Scientific American* ranks as the best source for reviewing the broad situation in a particular field, for interesting research problems that may produce future news stories and for graphic presentation of abstract concepts. *Science,* published by the American Association for the Advancement of Science in Washington, D.C., should be read each week.

Writers also read the British journals *Nature* and *The New Scientist* for new developments in research and policy. The nature of the scientific reporting system often "breaks" the news of research discoveries in the professional journals or at scientific meetings. Conflict exists between the journals and commercial trade magazines over publication; some journals refuse to publish a scientist's paper, for example, if any portion of it has appeared in print elsewhere. Sometimes this may hinder the science popularizer's efforts to obtain information on new developments in the laboratory.

Writers may scan many journals published by the various scientific fraternities. Earl Ubell says he receives more than 100 and could receive 900 more if he had the time to look through them (261:1). Since these articles are preevaluated by the scientists who edit the journals, the beginning writer can use these publications to confirm his own judgments about the material's news and scientific value. Exclusive stories never come easily. If digging through the journals produces them, the results are worth the time.

Background Knowledge Essential

Relations between scientists, doctor and writers have improved vastly in the past few years. One reason for this better exchange of information has been science's growing dependence on public support. Another reason is the willingness of writers to learn what the scientist or doctor is talking about. Many scientists and doctors will go through elementary explanations of their work, but the writer must demonstrate some knowledge of basic phenomena.

Dr. J.A. Beckmann of the Columbia University College of Physicians and Sureons has put it tersely for both the doctors and the scientists: "You talk the language or you waste the doctor's time with someone who simply doesn't understand the problem" (19).

The real test of a science writer's ability to make contact with his news sources does not occur at formal press conferences at a science or medical meeting. It does not come when a public relations man expends every effort to get the scientist to cooperate in an interview. It does not come in the writer's hometown where he may be known and respected as a local reporter. Blair Justice, award-winning science writer, declares:

The acid test, in my opinion, comes only when all these trimmings are stripped away and the reporter, completely unknown to the doctor, contacts the doctor directly and says: "I'd like to talk to you about your work" [122].

The writer's background also includes his knowledge or "feel" of the scientific method, the tools and the control of experimental research. The Council for the Advancement of Science Writing, Inc., attempts to locate scientists who will allow writers to spend vacation periods working with the researcher and to persuade newspaper executives to allow writers to stay with the scientist for a month or more to derive the maximum benefit (79).

Out of the reporter's background comes swift recognition of new stirrings in old research and the solution of classical problems. Real advances in science and medicine are seldom heralded with trumpets and cries of "breakthrough." (Scientists and science writers seem eager to forget that this word was ever applied to science.) Out of a reporter's background comes understanding of how and why fashions change in science and medicine.

This background, from reading and interviewing, enables a reporter to add historical perspective to his stories about current research. He learns of his Nobel laureates as the political writer learns of U.S. senators. He learns of the continuing conflicts within the scientific community and of the cathedrals of scientific knowledge and theory that are constantly being attacked and repaired.

The scene is always shifting. Pierre Fraley, former executive secretary to the CASW and a leading free-lancer, puts it this way:

Scientific knowledge is never final or complete, and I think the science writer would be doing a disservice to science if he gave the public the impression that when doctors or scientists agree about something (if they every do) that it then becomes an absolute and immutable truth. . . .

Science is not static. It is a serial in which each story has at the end "to be continued." It is only by showing the public that science is dynamic, is always examining, discovering, correcting, re-examining, adjusting, and extending knowledge that we will be meeting our responsibility in science reporting. Occasionally a report on even a bad piece of science can be useful in educating the public about the true aims and methods of science. It seems to me that this is the important area in which scientists, doctors, government officials, pharmaceutical firm executives, and science writers should be working together [59:66].

This represents an ideal, and ideal preparation for such a task is difficult to obtain. Science reporters absorb much of their background from their daily activities. John Troan, editor of the *Pittsburgh Press* and former president of NASW, summed up these interrelated activities (258:1194):

1. Reading of scientific journals and magazines.
2. Visiting research laboratories.
3. Attending background briefings by scientists of NASA, the Naval Observatory, Public Health Service, the National Bureau of Standards, scientific organizations and other public bodies.
4. Touring industrial laboratories during open houses and hearing lectures and witnessing demonstrations.
5. Attending science seminars sponsored by foundations, educational institutions and scientific societies.
6. Attending special institutes for science writers sponsored by the American Medical Association, National Association of Science Writers (NASW), the NSF, Rockefeller Institute and the Council for the Advancement of Science Writing. These short courses usually include a joint sponsorship by a science-writing group and one or more co-sponsors.

Troan has said that a hard-working, hard-reading science writer may acquire a broader knowledge of scientific activity in society and a better understanding of several related scientific fields than the scientist whose movements are more restricted.

Writing the Science Story

The time comes when you must sit down and write. By reading this far, you indicate some interest in writing science news. You may or may not pursue this speciality all of the time, but with the frequent scientific meetings and conventions around the country, likely no reporter can escape being asked to cover at least one of them.

Scientist and reporter alike should review one of the basic writing texts of the mass communications fields. Any science story can be fitted into the format of stories normally handled by newspapers, news magazines, magazines, television, radio, supplements and other periodicals. The subject may be science or scientists, but it must be written in the style normally employed by the medium.

The writer faces an immediate decision about the form in which he casts—or is forced to cast—his story. Because this choice determines what the writer says and how he says it, a swift review of these science story categories appears in order.

1. *News Story*: Brief, tersely written, factual account often hurriedly written or telephoned in following a speech or announcement in order to meet newspaper deadline or wire service competition.
2. *Feature Story*: Also called the "human interest" story, this permits the writer to present color, anecdote, detail, evidence or drama. It offers a more personal, intimate or human (focus on the people involved) story than the impersonal news account. More will be said about this later.
3. *Background Story*: All news and feature stories contain at least token background information. As a genre of news or newsfeature story, the "backgrounder" may trace events of days, years or even centuries leading up to a particular news event. It is often written in advance of a news event. A "backgrounder" can also present conflicts between authorities or organizations. This becomes increasingly necessary where science becomes identified with public policy (45:1).

4. *Interpretive Story* (sometimes called "Think Piece"): Allows author to state an opinion or others to take a position on the meaning of a news event. Sometimes this meaning is not clear and the meanings attached by various discussants are controversial. Like the background story, the interpretive calls for utmost care and checking of facts. Unless the writer is unusually well grounded in the topic, he will not write this kind of story in a hurry or without extensive research and interviewing.

5. *Column*: Usually reserved for Sunday or other regular publication day. the column offers more freedom for editorializing, comment and discussion in depth. It may not be attached to any news event.

6. *Personality Story*: Short biography to impart the spirit of the man of woman, how he works, his motivations, etc. Scientific information is secondary (239:193-200).

7. *Humor Story*: In science fields, a difficult type of article. Snickering pieces based on titled of papers or esoteric description of research grants are cheap burlesque. This will receive more attention later.

8. *Series*: A group of stories written about one topic because of its complexity or the need for breaking it down into brief parts; also a group of stories written around a central theme.

9. *Capsule Story*: A collection of brief, often varied items with little or no connection except that they may relate to science news.

10. *Situationer*: An article that says in effect, "This is where we stand today; this is the 'state of the art'." It usually outlines what is known and what is sought.

11. *Adventure in Science*: Margaret B. Kreig spent weeks in steaming jungles with botanists, doctors and pharmacists hunting new drug-bearing plants (128:1-446). She also dramatized accounts of expeditions, as told in the scientists' notebooks, to give this flavor of personal participation to the reader. David Perlman, *San Francisco Chronicle*, spent

two months as a member of the Galapagos International Scientific project. As an expedition member, he was asked to assist scientists in several research projects. "The idea was to write science for a change, where it was really happening—not out of the journals, nor out of the annual meetings, but out in the field . . ." (183:27).

Timing the appearance of your story is vital. Audience interest runs higher just before, during, or after a news event. Radio and television, naturally, can broadcast news events live, at the peak of interest for science-medical and other stories.

Reporters for both printed and broadcast media attempt also to "time" background, interpretative or situation stories to appear as close to the event as possible. Obviously, a thoroughly research-ed and well-written "backgrounder" just a day or two before the news event helps put the news in perspective, helps outline prob-lems and expected results and aids in understanding. The appear-ance of such information immediately after the event also in-creases reader understanding.

This need for timing requires the writer to anticipate news by several days, weeks and months in the case of some magazines. The intense planning and detailed work required for television productions requires similar advance thinking.

Sometimes anticipatory planning results in eerie coincidences. Howard Lewis on *Business Week*, for example, had been advised that medical researchers considered the time approaching when the first heart transplant would be attempted. He published a story giving the background of animal research, describing the most promising technique and its hazards. The story appeared on the same week end the first heart transplant was performed, December 3, 1967.

Ways of Writing the Story

Nothing beats knowledge of the subject in science writing or in any other field.

Skill and practice depend upon the individual. Nevertheless, experienced science writers offer many positive hints on how to attack the writing problem. Here are a few.

1. Science and medicine stories compete with all other stories for space; your story must be timely, interesting and understandable (4).
2. Try to tell your story in 800 to 900 words or less. Editors contacted by the World Book Encyclopedia Science Service prefer this length, equal to about one column of type. Wire services prefer 300 to 500 words. Anything longer becomes difficult to place in most newspapers and many magazines (220).
3. Illustrate stories whenever possible to increase understanding, another reason for keeping a story as short as possible to allow space for drawings or photographs.
4. Round off figures, remembering that in lay language there is no translation for the tenth decimal precision of mathematics in science (258:1194).
5. Employ analogy and word pictures to associate the often invisible, remote and unknown experiences in scientific research with a common, human experience (66:6).
6. Keep writing simple, clear, communicative and avoid writing down to your reader. It may help to conjure up a mental picture of some specific person you wish to reach (76:2).
7. Define unusual or technical terms and keep sentences short (76:5).
8. Get to the point immediately (76:10).
9. Translate the stiff, technical jargon of formal scientific papers and speeches; they often are badly written, poorly organized and presented to a captive audience (76:30).
10. Present one to three basic points per news story; interpretation of more than three "angles" requires a feature length piece (28:75).
11. Recognize the existence of more than one kind of "scientist"; differentiate between biologists, geologists, etc. (277:306).

12. Remember that new ideas in science do not always command instant acceptance. The findings of one scientist presented at a meeting may not be confirmed by other experimenters (259:3445).
13. Also remember that the Laws of Science are not like laws enacted for murder, rape and overtime parking. Scientific "laws" describe but they do not give a cause-and-effect explanation; when a phenomenon does not obey a supposed law of nature, the law must face revision (95:65).

Many positive statements may be made about science writing. Equally important are some negative guides. One of the most thorough lists of prohibitions comes from Science Service (224:3) in the science reporting business for 50 years. These include:

1. Don't overestimate the reader's knowledge, and don't underestimate his intelligence.
2. Don't try to tell all you know in 500 words. Leave some for another time.
3. Don't think that because a thing is old to you it is known to the public. Anything new to your readers is news to them if hung on a timely peg.
4. Don't forget that your reader is interrupting you every 10 lines to ask "Why?", "What for?" or Well, what of it?" and if you don't answer his tacit question, he will soon stop reading.
5. Don't think that you can make your topic more attractive by tricking it out with fairy lore or baby talk or irrelevant jokes or extravagant language.
6. Don't say "This discovery is interesting" unless you can prove it, and if you can prove it, you don't have to say it.
7. You don't have to give bibliographical references to all the literature on a subject, but don't fail to give the reader a clue he may use to begin more reading.
8. Don't expect an editor to explain why he objects to your manuscript. He is probably right in his verdict, but if you would make him give a reason for it, he will have to invent one and it would probably be wrong.

9. Don't define a hard word by a harder word.
10. Don't think you must leave out all the technical terms; use them when necessary, without apology and without a formal definition where possible. People aren't as easily scared by these words as you may think, and if you use the term in the correct way within the context of your story, it will be understood.

The Change in Pace

These helpful hints to science writing tell you nothing about how to begin any particular story. They may be regarded as buoys that ring bells or flash lights to inform the writer that he cruises along a broad channel whose limits are defined roughly. If you seek a formula for science stories, a variety may be found in texts on journalism. They illustrate ways many writers have found to pacify if not completely satisfy editors. (Writers keep these patterns in mind for those days when no unique, personal approach leaps to mind.)

The task, as set by Ruth Moore of *The Chicago Sun-Times* is to "try to interpret the work of scientists for the intelligent lay reader and draw it together into a connected story" (34:44).

How you do it is your business.

Earl Ubell advocates and practices the scrapping of the formula approach wherever possible.

"The news lead is dead; it is dead and dull. . . . The *who, what, where, when,* and *why* have been taught in every journalism school and class in the nation. Yet the net result has been to murder reading," he declared (261:3).

With style, drama, sharp words, unusual approach, bright phrase and above all the point of the story, Ubell attempts to hook his reader.

In one example of this technique, Ubell parodied a Chinese as he might have sounded while telling a friend about a science convention.

Great excitement yesterday at the Hotel New Yorker. . . . Upshot is that proton looks like a peach. Neutron like a lichee nut. Description may reveal in long run what holds universe together. Story starts with discovery of proton half century ago; neutron found thirty years ago [266:3] .

Ubell poked no fun at the importance of the discovery nor belittled the physicists' labors. Yet the reader derived pleasure as well as information from the telling. Obviously no one would write like this every day. However, Ubell was at one with Dr. Rudolph Flesch, a researcher in the art of readability, who praises the Chinese language style (75:14). Ubell's stripped-down writing style achieved a decent explanation of esoteric nuclear physics in less than 500 words. Brevity was the bonus, however, to the attempt to interest the reader.

Recently this author faced a similar situation in reporting the speech of a scientist specializing in (a) electron microscopy, (b) "macromolecules" and (c) biochemical processes of the brain. The story (37:1) split roughly into two parts. The first 150 words dramatized the scientist's battle to unlock the secret of giant molecules. The tone was that of a personal hand-to-hand combat between the scientist and his stubborn adversary. This opened the way to quoting the scientist on why he thought the battle was worth the effort and how he thought these particular chemical chains affected the brain's thought process. It was not done as well as Ubell's piece, but it satisfied a critical editor.

If you are energetic, you may mine more than one story a day. A news peg often presents itself so obviously you'd be foolish not to hang a story on it. Equally newsworthy at this same meeting were comments on the migration of European scientists to U.S. universities (39:1). Britain's "brain drain" was international news at that moment.

Try new approaches cautiously; editors understand politics and economics better than the sciences. Editors also like the old and familiar. Relating science stores to current events will win acceptance along with some freedom to experiment.

Tools of the Trade

Writers use many tools besides pencils and typewriters. Radio reporters and many television reporters use tape recorders to present their stories. More and more writers for the printed media find the recorder the best way of capturing exact quotes, the progress of an interview and the context of a question and answer exchange. Unlike notes, the tape does not become illegible after the reporter has worked on other stories.

Another tool, widely damned and praised, is the press release. Businesses, scientific societies, government offices, hospitals, research foundations, sociopolitical organizations, fund-raisers and a dozen other groups generate press releases by the bale.

Most go into the wastebasket.

The changing nature of scientific and engineering research makes the mail worth opening.

Reputable scientists usually publish first in society journals. Since acceptance and publication span weeks or months, alert publicists can coordinate an announcement with other institutions, scientists and government agencies. In the elaborate structure of science in the United States, such coordination avoids injured feelings among fellow scientists, institution management people, participants in cooperative efforts and, importantly, the foundations and government agencies which supply the money. Sometimes these orchestrations reach Wagnerian summits. When Dr. Arthur Kornberg announced the synthesis of DNA, the event was accompanied by a well-planned press conference on the West Coast and even rated a hastily-inserted mention in a speech being given by the President of the United States. A Canadian scientist wondered if scientists had become, perhaps, too skilled at press manipulation and were, perhaps, unprepared for such responsibility (222).

Science public relations offices can warn writers of announcements and their significance. This helps the writer prepare himself and estimate, for his editor, the size of the space or time needed later to tell the story. The PR officer can also help arrange interviews, illustrations and photography appointments.

Another tool a reporter can learn to use is the camera.

Walter Sullivan of *The New York Times*, for example, illustrated almost all of his stories about scientific research in the Arctic with his own photographs (245:41). Most newspapers and other publications hire professional photographers. These professionals should produce better pictures than the writer who takes photographs only as a part of his job. However, there are occasions when professionals are not available when the writer need them.

Another reason for taking your own pictures is expense. Publications will support the traveling expenses of one man, for instance, if he can provide both pictures and story. The expense of a photographer would strain the budget. In addition, many times only one man can be spared.

For trips to remote government installations where almost all supplies must ride in airplanes, the reporter often finds only one seat available. This author has converted hotel rooms, barracks closets and even his bunk and its layers of blankets into temporary darkrooms.

At times, special demonstrations are set up that cannot be duplicated without difficulty. Occasionally scientists will grant an interview but will not take additional time off for a photograph.

Scientists often appreciate extra photographs, and a free print of a picture may keep the laboratory door open.

Are Cameras Welcome?

In many places you cannot use a camera for good reasons.

Industrial research and development means money invested to pull ahead of a competitor. Companies eager to talk about their work often are not willing to have the processes or the machinery photographed. Many firms, particularly those on defense projects, collect all cameras at the front door. Don't feel you've been accused of sedition when you are asked to surrender your camera; often everyone who walks out of the building with a briefcase or shopping bag must be inspected. Armed services frequently impose such restrictions and security measures on their contractors to protect industrial and military secrets.

Electronic equipment used with some flash cameras can cause unwanted electrical disturbances in an area of delicate testing and experimentation. Also, many experimenters use explosive chemicals and gases (hydrogen or oxygen, for example). An electrical spark from a flashgun or an exploding flashbulb could ruin an experiment, the experimenter and all witnesses.

Speakers, and not scientists alone, will often object to the interruption of their talk by flashes of light in a darkened auditorium.

Does this mean you must pass up getting a picture. No. It places upon a writer the responsibility of planning for a photograph. Pictures can often be secured from public relations personnel or shot before or after a speech. In situations of corporate and military security restrictions, the company or the military can arrange to photograph a scene after making sure no compromise to security occurs.

"Pooling" of pictures and story information has become widely used by space science writers. On manned space flights, for instance, there are so many places where news occurs that one writer cannot possibly cover them all. For instance, how could a 600-man press corps of writers, photographers, radio broadcasters, television commentators and television cameramen shuttle between the "flight readiness room" at Cape Kennedy and the launching pad without creating confusion during very delicate preparations. Putting this many people around a fueled rocket when the astronaut enters his spaceship courts disaster.

Instead, the news services, some newspapers, magazines and television networks pool their manpower and equipment. This assures all media of at least one representative at each news point. These representatives produce pictures, facts and color at their individual locations. They file this information with NASA, whose information officers reproduce the pool copy for distribution. Any member of the radio or television pool can monitor all locations and broadcast the most interesting events. The cost is distributed among all pool members.

Doing His Job

The science writer always goes armed with the basic essentials to do his job. His knowledge, interest and intelligence constitute the most important factors in his performance, chiefly in the way in which he uses them.

Used skillfully, they can offset advantages of experience, influence and even opportunity in the case of science writers who work on smaller newspapers in suburban and medium-sized cities. To some extent, the rewards of science news develop in proportion to these qualities.

Let me cite two examples. I once sat on a jury selecting the winners of a medical writing contest. First place went to a writer from a small, upstate daily whose town had almost nothing in the way of advanced medical research although the general hospital facilities gave excellent medical care. The other writer ranked second, although his exhibit included several interviews with teachers and medical school researchers in his town. The first-place winner, we felt, drew much more readable and scientifically enlightening stories from limited resources than did the writer who dealt with men and women on the so-called "frontier of research."

Jerry Lochbaum, part-time science writer of the *San Antonio Express and News*, parlayed a simple story on the chemistry of flame into a runner-up award in the annual AAAS-Westinghouse Science Writing Awards contest.

Science writer Victor Cohn has offered these criticisms of current science news (53:751).

1. We spend the greater part of our time covering medicine; the general-science press corps has not yet caught up in excellence, numbers or hours.
2. We fail to pay enough attention to basic research and too often fire out news of new "discoveries" without connecting them with the main body of earlier knowledge.

3. We need to show more discrimination and moderation; we need to include qualifications early in the story and, we need to know more about interpreting—and questioning—statistics. "So do doctors—and scientists. They give us the news in the first place."

4. We are missing too many of the big stories through daily preoccupation with trivia; most of us don't find time for true, deep study.

5. Too many writers of science news releases overstate extravagantly; scientists and press officers do not hint that the same work may be going on at other places.

5
Covering the
Scientific Convention

The science writer will inevitably encounter a phenomenon known as "the scientific meeting." There are more than 200 scientific and engineering societies in the United States. There are a host of national, state and local medical societies. Nearly all of these assemble their members annually. When an almost unlimited number of special conferences, symposia and other meetings are added, one can see that almost any city may have one or more of these assemblies each month.

A few scientific conventions are overwhelmingly large. The American Association for the Advancement of Science regularly draws about 8,000 registrants for the week-long convention held each year during Christmas week. Because the AAAS membership includes many scientists and teachers affiliated with colleges and universities, these days between Christmas and New Years coincide with school vacations to help increase participation. The spring meeting of the Federation of American Societies for Experimental

Biology regularly presents more than 3,000 scientific reports. For the science writer, coverage becomes a matter of choosing the best material from such an offering.

In Washington, science writers experience "hell week" each spring. Meeting simultaneously are the National Academy of Sciences, the National Academy of Engineering, the International Scientific Radio Union, American Geophysical Union and the American Physical Scoeity. Members of the academies meet in one part of town, and the physicists gather far away in another part. Cooperation between the information officers of the three groups helps the science writers work much more confidently. The information officers arrange schedules of press conferences to avoid conflicts wherever possible.

On a recent occasion, press relations with a major society were injured badly because of communications failure. An aide received a call from a major scientific agency in the convention city. The government information man asked that the dozens of science writers at the meeting be told of a press conference to announce the closing of an important laboratory. For reasons still unclear, no notice was posted; most of the writers were beaten on a story happening only a few blocks away.

Assembling many experts in one place naturally makes for a newsworthy situation. Many newsmen, magazine writers and book authors attend the meetings to confer with scientists about stories already being written, to get ideas for future stories and to meet the experts and arrange to visit them. This ease in meeting and communicating with one's own colleagues explains in part the popularity of the scientific conventions.

Conventions and News

Tradition and ethics require most scientists to reveal their latest research discoveries to other scientists before making public pronouncements. The professional scientific journal and the annual scientific meeting provide recognized channels for such presentations. In both instances the scientist goes before his peers with an argument and supporting data intended to satisfy the standards of his fellow experts. He goes "on the record," so to speak, before the scientific community.

The scientific meeting generates more news than publication in a scientific journal since the journals often lag behind the researchers. Despite this delay, "publication by press release" subjects the scientist to censure by his peers and damages his professional standing. In fairness to the scientific publications, it should be noted that the editors of journals realize the problems of delay and strive to increase the currency of their articles. So, the journal should not be abandoned completely in favor of convention news as a source of popularized science stories. Often the paper at the convention represents an updating of journal results.

Some papers coincide with publication in the society's journal. Thus the scientist makes himself available to elaborate on the article. Scientists in convention may also deliver papers that refute or confirm the findings of colleagues presented in the journals or in earlier convention papers.

The convention satisfies one news element. Any convention story can contain those three little words that unlock the heart of a city editor and consequently space in the newspaper. The words: "said here today." They reassure the editor that while he may not be publishing eternal truths he has a topic that is here, and now, and local. The convention is "live."

Covering a scientific meeting offers some obstacles and some benefits not usually found at, say, a convention of Lions Clubs, the gathering of politicians or an assembly of businessmen. In a typical scientific meeting, the writer's judgment of what is news hinges on many factors including the physical task of getting around to literally hundreds of different sessions. This takes some planning, especially when one apparently interesting meeting conflicts with another held at the same time and often in another building.

Another problem involves competition between writers and media. Seldom has the author found fewer than 10 to 15 other newsmen present at a scientific meeting. Sometimes the communicators threaten to outnumber the delegates.

Recently some informal ground rules for scientific press relations have been organized, published and circulated for the benefit
of both parties. The best discussions of both policy and techniques
at the convention are found in two booklets, *Science News Communication* and *Scientist, Meet the Press* (215).

The first handbook comes from the National Association of
Science Writers and details the ideal situation that NASW members
prefer at a scientific meeting. The other was prepared by the
Smith Kline and French Laboratories to guide its scientific staff.

For the general reporter and the specialist, successful coverage
of science and scientists will depend heavily upon how well they
understand and use a variety of techniques. These techniques apply equally well, with some variations, for situations dealing with
such semiscientific government organizations as NASA or the
NSF.

Advance Notices

Seldom does a scientific meeting arrive as any surprise. Members receive notices of the meeting, make room reservations and
begin preparation of papers several months in advance. Convention
bureaus in the host city, local scientists and many other people get
involved in the preparations.

Notices of meetings printed for months in advance can be
found in any issue of such publications as *Science, Aviation Week*
and *Physics Today*.

The national headquarters of an organization, such as the
American Chemical Society, probably will send city editors, news
editors and science writers one or more publicity notices. The
national headquarters will also provide an advance schedule or
program two or three weeks before the meeting.

If the meeting is coming to the writer's town, members on the
local arrangements committee can advise him of interesting and
significant papers. Securing advance programs helps focus attention on local scientists, or famous ones, who will present papers.

Armed with such advance notice, a writer can secure interviews with local people and find out early what they will be saying and the significance of their work. Careful attention to the advance program and following up on information therein avoids the sometimes embarrassing event of having a wire service reporter from elsewhere, say, Chicago or New York, come booming in first with a story about scientists from the reporter's home city.

One word of caution should be sounded on the use of the advance program. A scientist may or may not want to talk about his paper. He may, rightfully, ask you not to publish any story about his paper or research until the paper is delivered. The ability to make advance preparation on such a story makes it worthwhile to agree to these wishes. By honoring the release time, one ensures that future dealings with the news source will be friendly.

If the convention is out of town, the local scientist may give the reporter a copy of his paper for release on the day of its delivery. Probably he will go over the paper, explain its technical language and discuss implications of the research and how his work fits into the larger pattern of research in his field. He may even ask assistance in writing a "lay language" abstract for the convention pressroom.

More and more often planners of scientific meetings are asking participants to send popularized versions of significant papers. These are duplicated and placed in the pressroom.

Organizations experienced in dealing with newsmen's requests insist more and more that the scientist provide the text in time for reproduction and distribution. The American Institute for Aeronautics and Astronautics, for example, does a profitable trade in selling preprints of all papers at the national and regional conferences. Newsmen get copies without charge.

Other organizations print abstracts of papers in their programs or in a special booklet distributed at the meeting. The reporter should find out where and how preprints of the meeting will be available. Some will be meaningless to him. Some scientists consulted in advance of a convention confess that their colleagues write such vague abstracts that they themselves cannot judge the potential importance of the paper.

Scientists are human, and some will not write their papers until the last minute. Some will not even appear at the meeting for various reasons. And other scientists will withdraw their papers for reasons that may range from failure to write it to a last-minute discovery that their project has been a total failure. Therefore, the schedule must be double-checked for last-minute changes.

Using the Pressroom

Pressrooms and their facilities vary considerably. So does the caliber of the people who run them. However, only a few organizations today fail to make provisions for newsmen. At a very minimum the registration clerks will issue the working newsman a convention badge, enabling him to move freely among the delegates.

On other occasions the author has found pressrooms locked throughout a meeting and the scientist appointed to run it hidden somewhere in the audience listening to the speeches. However, he has found such scientists—when located—very willing to assist.

Any newsman, and certainly the science specialist, should possess the initiative to overcome such a handicap, if it be a handicap. One can always approach the speaker himself or seek guidance from the chairman. These examples are cited merely to illustrate the variance from the ideal that exists.

In general the proud tradition of open discussion in the scientific society continues today. The meetings usually are open to the public, sometimes for a registration charge, as well as to the press. At semiscientific meetings, usually sponsored by military or paramilitary organizations, some or all sessions may be open only to persons with a security clearance. It is the writer's responsibility to acquaint himself with such conditions as far in advance as possible.

One person usually has complete charge of the pressroom. He may be a scientist temporarily detailed to this job. If he is a scientist, he usually seems to be one whose relations with the press have been cordial in matters dealing with his own research. Often the press officer is a public relations man from the society's staff or from a firm hired for the occasion.

One should inquire about the amount of assistance the press officer can give. Some will arrange interviews; other leave it up to the reporter to contact scientists for extended discussion.

If the meeting attracts enough reporters, the press office may provide telephones, copy paper and carbons. Otherwise, the reporter should bring his own.

Some pressrooms offer a few reference books, and occasionally the society hires an official photographer for use by science writers. A thoughtful press officer will have photographs of major speakers, file copies of as many papers as possible and duplicating equipment to reproduce these papers if writers request complete texts.

If there are major dinner and luncheon speakers, the press officer usually has tickets. Generally, but not always, these tickets are free to working newsmen; a writer should not expect these free tickets, however, and should be prepared to pay his way. Too many free press tickets, for instance, could damage the budget of a small society.

Scientific societies conduct some newsworthy business. They elect officers, confer awards and pass resolutions. These make news, and the press officer should be contacted on these possibilities.

Conference papers rank below printed journal articles in status. A speech, naturally, does not permit leisurely study, detailed analysis and testing of the reported results. Scientists may present only the most interesting slice of their work. When they publish later for the permanent record in the science literature, more extensive experiments may modify or even reverse conclusions presented at the meeting. Yet the delay involved in actually getting a report into a journal makes an oral report attractive; it sometimes offers a researcher his best chance to call new work to scientific and public attention. This situation is always changing, however. Certainly the scientist who distributes a 6,000-word text of his speech through the pressroom is "published" in the very real sense of being on record (47).

Handling of Texts

The availability of texts of speeches varies with any given scientific meeting. Some societies, such as the American Institute of Physics, attempt to provide mimeographed copies of every paper and sometimes a popularized text as well; others maintain a master file of papers for use by writers.

Scientists employed by private industry, foundations, many government agencies and some universities have their own public relations office strike copies for the press.

Industrial public relations men often flood the pressroom with news releases, photographs and other material that may or may not relate to the conference. There's one way to deal with this material; read it and throw it away unless it fits into a current or future story. The industrial PR man can arrange interviews with his company's scientists attending the meeting.

Most societies adhere to the newspaper and television release times recommended by the National Association of Science Writers. Papers delivered before 1 p.m. are released automatically to afternoon newspapers published on the day the papers are presented. Papers presented after 1 p.m., local time, are released for the morning of the following day.

Other groups, and often individual scientists, prefer a more precise release time. This usually coincides with the anticipated time of delivery. The policy should be stated in the official program, in a notice posted in the press room, or in an attachment to the paper. For example, the paper or press release may be tagged: "Hold for Release until 9 a.m., May 8," or "Release upon Delivery."

Writers may telegraph stories to their newspapers based upon such papers and notify editors that these stories are to be held for release. When risking such items to chance publication in advance of delivery, the writer must be certain that the scientist actually delivers the address.

Press Conferences

Scientific press conferences are a delight. They save newsmen from confusion and produce much of the understanding that comes from a convention. Unlike the political press conference usually called to announce news, the scientific press conference aims at explaining and amplifying what the scientist said in his convention paper. Here the scientist can set the record straight on what he wants the press to see in his work and what he does not want writers to attribute to it. He may discuss how he performed his experiments and his personal reaction to his work.

The scientist may unbend, couch his explanations in lay analogies, discuss his family life and reveal his hopes for the future. He may open new controversies and express extraneous opinions.

A press officer may schedule conferences for the press with scientists whose papers appear to have high news value. The reporter should watch for such schedules posted in the pressroom.

Often a "sleeper" paper produces a demand for a press conferences. News that occurs outside the convention may generate requests from the press corps for comment and interpretation from spokesmen for the society or from one or more scientists as individuals.

The press conference may involve only one scientist. Often several scientists participate if they are members of a research team or panel members who have presented a group discussion on several aspects of a topic.

Press conference material falls under the same rules as the release of scientific papers. A press conference to develop information about a paper that is for "future" release—tomorrow, for instance—remains tied to the release time of the paper or discussion. If the paper is to be delivered before 1 p.m., the press conference material is likewise embargoed for afternoon release.

There is one exception agreed upon by the NASW. When a press conference reveals "extraordinary news," writers need not hold back. Carefully the NASW members refuse to vote any hard-and-fast definitions of what constitutes "extraordinary news." For the inexperienced who may not be able to distinguish between normal reportorial noise and that which signals "extraordinary news," a few quick questions to other newsmen will clear up any confusion.

Manned landings on the moon, synthesis of genetic materials, heart transplants and other spectacular "firsts" in science have expanded the use of special treatment for "extraordinary news."

Space flights and the recovery of a heart transplant patient are reported as events take place. The space agency assembles special scientific meetings and allows writers to get the reports of scientific tests, such as those conducted on rocks from the moon at the same time they are given to the scientific community. Other scientists consider their discoveries significant enough to obtain permission for a public announcement soon after their peers review and accept the research report for journal publication.

The conduct of the reporter at a press conference determines how valuable the session is to him. The subject should not have to act as an umpire for the questions of a dozen or so reporters. This chore often becomes that of the press officer and sometimes that of the scientific panel's chairman or a senior journalist. Everyone present should have an opportunity to question the subject as thoroughly as required. However, the scientist is not required to answer questions that are stupid, impertinent or obviously aimed at embarrassing him. The scientist may offer personal and professional opinions. He discusses the commercial and policy developments of his company, if he works for an industrial laboratory, or the activities beyond his own level in government at his personal risk. Seldom does one person speak for all other scientists.

For further discussion of these matters, the two booklets mentioned earlier should be reviewed; they are the source for this material.

Victor Cohn, science editor for *The Washington Post,* has called the press conference one of the most important aspects of covering a scientific convention (58:4). It is second only to reading the complete text of the scientific paper, he feels, and writers and scientists should attempt to expand the use of both techniques.

Private Interviews

The availability of press conferences should not discourage a reporter from seeking private interviews. As mentioned, the presence of so many experts invites a writer to use his imagination and initiative to uncover new stories. Personal interviews may be arranged by contacting the scientist after his talk through messages on the convention bulletin board or by a call to the scientist's room. Press officers often arrange interviews on request. One should not be surprised, however, to find that the request for a personal interview produces a general press conference. Several individual requests may persuade the press official to call the scientist to a news conference rather than have him repeat the same material in several interviews. However, the personal interview remains another way to secure the exclusive story offering depth, clarity and interpretation through a thorough discussion.

Medical stories should emphasize that the doctor being quoted is "one single doctor, one single man," says Dr. James B. Donaldson of the Philadelphia County Medical Society (81:46).

Lee Linder of the Associated Press holds that doctors are seldom misquoted but often regret their words "when associates tell them they should have kept their mouths shut" (81:46).

Science writers usually note in their stories which material came from a press conference or personal interview. This, as demonstrated by Robert K. Plumb, benefits understanding by the readers who may observe that the scientist's formal speech did not contain some of the printed material (186). The same caution applies to telephone interviews. In many cases of newsworthy research, the American Institute of Physics, for one, will notify writers of an article in print. The society provides the writer with the scientist's telephone number and arranges for the researcher to answer calls from writers.

Dr. Phillip Abelson, editor of *Science,* dislikes news coverage outside the articles published in journals. He warns reporters to beware of the scientist "operator."

Today, newspaper reporting of new developments makes it possible for scientific "operators" to circumvent science's methods of self-policing. The publicity-seeker can give his story direct to reporters. Newspapers do not print sufficient technical detail to permit other scientists to confirm the facts behind an announcement. Even if they did, and the story were proven false, the "operator" could shrug his shoulders and say he was misquoted.

A similar problem arises when reporters cover scientific meetings. Many of the verbal presentations never subsequently appear in print. Speakers are not so careful about being rigorous when they know that their words are not permanently on record. Some are deliberately careless and slant their talks so as to attract publicity. Scientists who have soberly reported substantial advances find their work ignored as not being exciting enough.

Using shrewd tactics an "operator" can establish himself as a newsworthy person. This can open the road to research grants and even academic advancement. Only a few scientific specialists will suspect that he is a phony, and they will have no practical mechanism for penalizing him [59:17-19].

Relation to News Sources

Reporters over the years have established personal relationship with information sources. This is true in science writing, particularly where the source retains almost complete control over the information. These conclusions about this relationship come from Smith, Kline and French (215:4), a drug firm whose scientists deal regularly with the science writers:

1. The specialist writer often feels a closer kinship to the scientist than to fellow journalists.
2. The specialist usually respects the scientist's traditional caution and objectivity more than the general reporter.
3. Specialists tend to extrapolate or extend research data from animals to humans with more caution than does the general reporter.
4. Science writers usually "talk the language" and assist in the communications problem. In short, there is a genuine effort to respect each other's competence.

Requests by scientists to go "off-the-record" occur frequently enough that the NASW has been very specific in its advice to members and scientists. Each "off-the-record" comment must be prefaced by this warning, and any statement not so heralded will be considered back "on the record." Sometimes scientists really mean that information is "for background only," meaning reporters are being given the material to understand a situation, not for direct quotation. Other information may be on a "not for attribution" basis, meaning you may not quote the source.

Writers often meet special "peer pleadings" from scientists. The scientist feels he cannot explain his work for laymen; he considers his field so specialized that only another scientist is competent to understand and judge the work.

This poses delicate situations for writers. This author, with embarrassment, recalls several instances when he pressed a scientist to explain some very esoteric research. Often the result confirmed the scientist's opinion that the work had no interest for the public. So, no story. On other occasions, the scientist did not wish to cooperate, and the discussion was so technical or abstruse that the writer was unable to comprehend and question. Also, no story.

Out of several hundred interviews, however, this has not been the usual experience. In general, a demonstration of real interest in a scientist's work, coupled with a rudimentary grasp of technical terms, will produce at least a lukewarm response. Scientists possess the human desire for understanding and appreciation of their work.

Any situation involving "peer pleadings" probably means one is dealing with a "hostile witness," for lack of a better term. A writer cannot force such a man to talk, and unless they strike some mutually satisfactory response, the writer probably will fare better with someone else.

Such a scientist complicates the reporting problem when he controls public funds or operates in areas of controversy and high public interest. The decision to press such a scientist, usually a government official, for more information may hinge upon weighing the man's actions as a scientist against his post as a public official.

Showing the story

Should a reporter show his story to a scientist?

Requests to do so come often to the science writer. The subject may arise as casually as an offer to check the story for accuracy, or it may be stated as a demand. Some scientists grant interviews only on the condition that they read what is written.

The writer is not obliged to show his story to any news source unless he has promised to do so as a condition for being given the material. If he should allow a review as the condition to an interview, he should honor his commitment.

Many reasons argue against committing oneself to a story review by anyone except the editor. Newspapers and news magazines seldom have the time for a review before publication. Features, perhaps, could be checked, but there is no chance to review stories written to meet hour-by-hour deadlines.

The writer who submits his story for review cannot guarantee, except with the agreement of others, that the story will appear as approved. If he accepts a commitment to a story review, it should be done with the permission of his editor. Stories are rewritten frequently; on news magazines and many newspapers and magazine supplements, the printed story frequently results from writers boiling down and shaping facts filed by a reporter.

Scientists also exhibit a very human quality when given a reporter's story. An "accuracy only" check often turns into a semiliterary brannigan over news judgment, writing style and approach. A few scientists can improve these qualities. More often, however, the technical specialist will impersonalize the story and substitute technical terms for acceptable and more human analogies. Only a few scientists can switch literary styles from the technical to the lay language essential to newspaper articles.

Writers for general feature magazines may afford the luxury of submitting a story or a proof to a news source. These stories go through many revisions in normal production; often they are written weeks before the deadline, and the deadline itself is weeks before publication.

As a practical matter, science and medical news writers often check with the news source for the technical accuracy of fact and analogy. The practice helps preserve good will and cooperation. It saves the reporter and his news source from criticism for error. There are several techniques short of committing the publication to printing only the version initialed by the news source. All of these techniques are geared to the time available.

Reporters should check key facts in an advanced text against the scientist's oral presentation. The writer may telephone the news source when he feels uncertain about the accuracy of his own wording. Reporters should also check other facts against encyclopedias or standard references. Sometimes writers show the news source a carbon copy of the story. With the original in the hands of the city deskmen, accuracy becomes the only basis for change.

On rare occasions the story may be important enough to submit to a scientist for publication only with his approval. Occasionally the reporter may develop a story, perhaps even "ghosting" the story, for the scientist's by-line in a newspaper.

Who Decides What's News?

"The doctor and I reached an agreement on separation of responsibilities," a medical writer said recently. "He'll decide when patients are sick. I'll decide when they are news" (22:137).

A president of the Associated Press Managing Editors once said: "How does the newspaper editor know how to judge what's news in science unless he's part scientist? He doesn't" (160:7).

Ultimately the job rests on the science writer whose specialist position makes him the *de facto* science news advisor. This task comes hardest during a scientific meeting. Unless the session is limited to only a few papers, complete coverage is impossible. The writer must select, judge and emphasize the topics that are news in his publication.

The easiest story to get from any meeting is an account of one man's work. Some papers are obvious newsmakers. The subject matter or the results sound "newsy." Unless the speaker presents a broad view, he usually reports only on a single fragment of research. The writer may need to secure additional background information. Sometimes the unusual amount of work involved or the man may qualify for a story, however unimportant or impractical his research.

Sometimes the lack of a "finding" may qualify for a story. When 26-year-old Albert A. Michelson and Edward W. Morley, 42, found no variances in the speed of light through the earth's ether, they set the stage for Albert Einstein and his theory of relativity. The test produced an important "negative result" (109).

The press director of a meeting can give an estimate of the significance of a piece of research. Writers also seek expert opinion from other scientists at the meeting. Their thoughts and quotes can open the way for the writer to present an expert evaluation of a researcher's methods, the effects of a report upon scientists and any speculation on the significance and ramifications of a report. This was the method Wil Lepkowski of McGraw-Hill World News used (145:5) to pin down a strange new effect observed by physicists.

The Local Delegation

Scientists from many cities generally participate in a science program. Often a scientist from the reporter's city will present a paper at the meeting. The science writer, like the political writer at a national convention, faces this question: What do you report about the local delegation?

If the writer has done his homework, likely he has already secured copies of all the local scientific reports. Before the meeting he knows whether or not his local scientists will report anything newsworthy. Probably he has already written some local stories and has left them with the city desk, marked "Hold for Release."

Many editors still hold to the axiom: "All news is local news." In this parochial view, a few newspapers want lists of everyone from the newspaper's city who is attending the meeting. Wire service reporters sometimes chew through stacks of scientific papers to produce a string of short stories for distribution on the regional wires to local newspapers.

The high price of newspaper space forces most metropolitan editors to use the "local news" rules with a reverse axiom: "All that's local is not news." The local scientist makes copy only when he has something new to say. Do not interpret this to mean that the local scientist becomes valueless unless he delivers the convention's best paper. Hometown scientists may win office or may receive awards for service. One should check the local scientists in advance for such news and watch for developments during the meeting. Since most newspapers serve a large circulation area, the "local' scientist also includes people within the newspaper's territory. When the reporter files to a local-minded city editor, the local scientists can become valuable "scientific consultants" to the writer. They can provide background, evaluation and perspective on scientific and political issues.

Local delegates may seem more approachable away from home in the convention atmosphere. Scientists, too, have their cocktail hours; but one should be wary of using any scientific information gleaned in periods of alcoholic conviviality. To use such high-powered speculation as gets kicked around on the party circuit invites alienation of local sources, the loss of some very interesting party invitations and inevitably a tough time explaining to the city editor why the world's greatest science story was wrong. The cocktail-oriented science story must be checked back with the source the next morning—if it still sounds newsworthy.

Aiding the Editors

Art J. Snider of *The Chicago Daily News* (229:2) says the science writer can guide copy editors and other deskmen to make better choices from among the stories offered each day. During the week of March 8, 1964, Snider counted 58 science stories filed by the local staff and wire services to his newspaper. The editors printed eight stories about the "frills of science," without seeking an opinion from the science writer. Snider's experience suggests that the science writer should prepare his city desk and perhaps the wire or copy desks for significant developments coming out of science meetings. An advisory may take the form of a memo in advance of the meeting. No newspaper expects one reporter to write every story of a large convention, and such an advisory can assist news editors in judging material flowing in from as many as a dozen wire services.

Sometimes reporters make news judgments on a very personal basis. Jack Smith of *The Cincinnati Enquirer* considers that his years of experience have developed a "following" for his science news. With this in mind, he says he covers "only what interests me" (227). When the writer is truly attuned to his local audience, the method is excellent. When the writer's interests are broad, as with Smith, the stories catch an audience's attention swiftly.

Even for the beginning science writer this method has some reason; for one thing, "what interests me" presumes some understanding of the subject by the writer. This familiarity may prevent many unconscious errors and false assumptions. However, the strict application of such a formula—or any formula—has serious drawbacks.

Successful application of the above principle depends upon the reporter's ability to sense a true picture of what happens at a given time and place. If a reporter "likes" the wrong things, there is a good chance that a false impression will be created by his stories and will never be corrected. The report depends upon the reporter; he may do better asking, "What is important in it all?"

Even in science the competition often dictates what news one selects to cover. One of the first questions the beginning reporter must face is, "Who are we out to beat?" Local newspaper competition decreases with the increase of one-newspaper towns. Where newspaper ownership is divided, even on a morning-evening basis, the other newspaper generally becomes the foremost competitor. For spot news, writers must provide greater depth and clarity to meet competition from radio and television stations; these media distribute many news items before the printing process can get underway.

Radio and television reporters, even in science news, receive precious air time for documentary films and extended interviews that often prove more dramatic and interpretive than a story. In the opinion of his editor, Jules Bergman of the American Broadcasting Company does extremely well in managing the time and technical considerations necessary to produce first-rate science and technology programs. Bergman stresses the job's difficulties from the time, energy and vast amounts of cooperation required from scientists in staging the television productions devoted to science.

Television and radio competition challenge the writer to get the story first through advance, personal interviews and by finding original stories not listed on the meeting program. Secondary competition develops among the writers attending the meeting. When a dozen or more writers cover the same events, they compete for best treatment of information as well as for exclusive stories. The friendly rivalry in no way prevents writers from exchanging information, consulting with others or comparing notes to confirm the accuracy of fact and quotation.

Real competition comes also from the wire services, large regional dailies and news magazines. The reporter's meeting stories must compete with stories from various wire services for publication. This competition may be considered a battle for the mind of the editor. And as noted earlier, the editor does not necessarily use the same standards as may govern the choices of the writer or the scientist.

Getting the Story Home

Meeting and beating the competition can depend on how well one understands the mechanics of communication. Each newspaper, for instance, has its own preferred practices and individual deadlines.

"Press telegram" remains a common way of getting the story back home, although rates no longer favor this method. More wire service and newspaper reporters are sending stories over new "light transmission" or "optical scanner" equipment.

Many newspapers have installed recording rooms as telephone rates have become increasingly competitive with press telegram rates. The reporter dials a tape recorder phone and dictates his story. Secretaries or other reporters transcribe the story. The procedure reduces the time needed to get the story into the office. Fastbreaking news demands use of the telephone to reach the city desk or a rewrite man directly. Rarely does science news demand such high-speed priority except for extremely important local news or in a very competitive situation. In these circumstances, reporters should telephone the story long enough before deadline to permit the rewrite man and the desk to type, edit and headline the story.

Seldon is a long story dictated by telephone. Usually the telephone is used for a short but important report which becomes a new "top" or "lead" to a story filed earlier.

The release times placed on scientific papers take much of the rush out of newspaper deadline activity. Because release times are fixed, the stories can be wired in well ahead of time. However, the reporter should guard against new developments, including the possibility that a paper may be suddenly withdrawn.

In many situations pictures or drawings needed to illustrate stories can be obtained. Special transmissions, at extra cost, can be arranged through the wire services' picture networks. Often the wire services themselves will file the same picture or a similar one, and reporters should alert the news desk to watch for the suitable picture.

Often the reporter may secure exclusive pictures or may take his own. The photographs, drawings or unprocessed film should be sent air mail or air express. The package should also contain unmistakable identification of the pictures, including full names of the people. The editor should be advised that this material is coming. If it is sent by air express, the editor needs to know the flight number and arrival time to assign someone to pick it up at the airport.

After the Convention

What happens when the scientific meeting closes? As in other conventions, the delegates scatter as soon as possible. The science reporter also has business waiting for him elsewhere. Does this mean the meeting is dead now?

For the science reporter the answer is "no."

As mentioned, the variety of topics discussed at the average scientific meeting forbids complete coverage. Only the best papers and the more interesting topics get immediate attention.

However, many research papers are saved because they contain valuable background material. Any scientific meeting contains many papers that are insignificant by themselves. However, the sum of these papers may constitute a solid "situation" report in a field of research. For example, the annual American Association for the Advancement of Science symposia on arid lands represents such a case.

This author collects papers about unusual animals used for experiments. Others collect isolated research papers that fit stories planned for the future.

These papers represent source material for major feature stories or for a future science column. They also may remind the writer about research of potential future interest and of news contracts.

David Perlman of *The San Francisco Chronicle* finds other uses for papers by scientists in California, Washington, Nevada and Utah (182). Although many of these reports lack immediate news value, he uses them as the basis for a visit to the scientists later. The papers give him background for personal interviews.

Once the rush of the scientific meeting has passed, writers analyze the papers for leads to future stories. Some papers demand an immediate follow-up. Walter Sullivan of *The New York Times* heard scientists describe how land life survives following a volcanic eruption. The conference took place in Honolulu. On his return to New York, Sullivan developed the story through a telephone interview (246:21).

Bonus Stories

On this same Honolulu trip Sullivan covered the tenth Pacific Science Congress, remaining in the islands almost a month. The conference lasted two weeks. After the conference closed, Sullivan filed a variety of stories dealing with research by scientists in Hawaii. These included a report on Smithsonian Astrophysical Observatory personnel who photograph satellites and on a University of Hawaii team interested in the dim light called "Gegenschein" (243:17). He also visited meterologists and geophysicists living and working atop Mauna Loa volcano (242:29).

It is common practice for science writers covering an annual meeting to gather other stories during the dull parts of a meeting or on their way back home. This practice broadens the science coverage offered the newspaper reader. From the standpoint of economics, the writer provides a larger file of science stories at the price of one basic travel expense.

Arrangements should be made with the institutions visited as far in advance as possible to make sure that the people the reporter wants to see will be available.

6
Three Principles of Usefulness

"Why do we need a science writer?"

The question came in an unusual burst of candor from a newspaper colleague. Over another beer he expounded his favorite theory that "any good reporter should be able to handle any story."

The Houston Chronicle printed an effective answer less than a week later. About 4 p.m., August 20, 1964, the mayor of Houston announced that the city apparently was gripped by an epidemic of mosquito-borne encephalitis. Despite the fact that *The Chronicle's* last edition was off the press, everyone went into action. The general reporters and the medical writer went to the official press conferences. In addition, the medical writer called her physician news-sources to get estimates other than the official one on the size and extent of the outbreak. The science writer began hunting local authorities on mosquitoes and their habits.

The medical writer, Mrs. Moselle Boland, prepared a sidebar to the encephalitis story detailing the history of encephalitis, its symptoms, the usual course of the disease, the possibilities of contracting the disease and the probable length of time required for recovery (31:8).

The science writer's sidebar detailed the unique breeding places of those mosquitoes most likely to carry the disease, their peculiar habits of living and reproducing, the most likely source of the virus and how mosquitoes transfer the infection to people (41:9).

The incident illustrates the first of three "principles of usefulness" that guide science writers outside the strict "news of science" category.

The First Principle

Principle 1. Support and interpret general news coverage for your publication.

Earl Ubell, science editor of *The Herald Tribune,* was one of the finest practitioners of this technique. Following a particularly sordid murder, Ubell opened his story thusly:

> Strange as it seems, the man who murdered and sexually abused four-year-old Edith Kiecorius may be legally and psychiatrically sane. This is the consensus of psychiatrists interviewed yesterday by this department [262:1].

Similarly *The Houston Chronicle* developed an exclusive evaluation of the first close-up pictures of the moon. Interviews with several leaders of Project Apollo revealed for the first time how doubtful many were of the manned landing and their relief over interpretations of the photographs (44:8).

The science writer develops a particular set of contacts for stories only slightly related to science. A casual conversation with a marine biologist about his research institute revealed some doubts about the plans of The University of Texas for the institution. Later a friend mentioned that a French telescope expert had moved to Texas' McDonald Observatory. A very satisfactory news-feature story dealing with new plans for the two scientific installations resulted from following up these bits of information.

The Second Principle

Miss Dusty Vineberg, medical writer for *The Montreal Star,* says, "You get story ideas from almost everything you do" (272:38). A writer fits his work to the pattern of the organization employing him. This brings us to the second principle of usefulness in science writing.

Principle 2. Provide scientific information, as stories or notes, to other departments.

"Let me have that when you're through with it," said Bob Brister, leafing through an oceanography report from the University of Miami, Florida. "I want to make a column out of this."

Brister, outdoors writer for *The Houston Chronicle,* was excited by the account of a research cruise. The oceanographers apparently had located the long-sought spawning grounds of swordfish and sailfish and had brought back the smallest-known specimens, perfectly formed babies only an inch long.

Scientific investigation is so extensive that it is a cliche to say scientists are dealing with every aspect of the world. Yet, the science writer must demonstrate it to others.

> Science belongs to everyone. This is a point that may fail to occur to some editors who long have been accustomed to equating reader interests with proximity to where the news happened [118:10].

This belief was expressed by Blair Justice, a writer who places science material in various departments of the newspaper.

One of Justice's stories, for instance, appeared on the front page of *The Houston Post's* business section. It discussed how scientific techniques move into commercial use after laboratory development (121:1).

Moselle Boland of *The Houston Chronicle* prepared a color spread for the rotogravure section. The picture story, "Modern Art in Nature" (30:10-11), consisted of microscope photographs of polio virus, virus from a monkey's kidney and a diseased cell from a cow.

Editors of the art and culture sections also become involved in scientific stories from time to time. Electronic music, of course, requires the music critic's ear to evaluate it, but the subject also should intrigue the writer attuned to science and mathematics. A new scientific technique proved that an almost revered example of Etruscan sculpture at the Metropolitan Museum of Art was a forgery (24:1).

Women's pages form a natural market for scientific stories relating to physical and mental health, family care and new "wonder-gadgetry" for the home.

At the annual International Home Furnishings Market, women's writer Harriet Morrison remarked: "What a reporter needs to cover this market is an up-to-date chemistry handbook" (158:16).

Women scientists fill the constant demand for women-at-work profiles and biographical studies.

Hobbies, entertainment and recreation departments also offer lodging for science stories. Jack Gould of *The New York Times,* for example, devoted a radio column to the effect of sunspots and the earth's disturbed ionosphere upon amateur and commercial broadcasting (158:15).

Medical stories, which may be considered as applied biology and biochemistry, appear in various departments. Readership is guaranteed on almost any medical report, but special placement often can insure nearly 100 percent attention.

Many newspapers have changed the style and format of their society or women's pages to admit more solid news and feature material. Partly this reflects increased respect for women's reading tastes and partly the commercial side of "unisex" thinking. No editorial manager really likes to contemplate the entire male portion of his audience, automatically discarding a third or a fourth of the product. During Congressional hearings devoted in 1970 to the various medical dangers associated with the use of birth control pills, many science writers found their news stories, interpretative articles and features about "The Pill" used in the women's sections. The stories were read by men, too, with and without urging from their wives or girl friends. Likewise, the warnings about dangerous cosmetics, health fads, medical frauds and household chemicals move toward these special interest pages.

In some of the tougher real estate sections, science writers may dig into the scientific causes of certain natural quirks in local geology. These affect real estate values and guide the selection of home sites in some areas. Certain clays suddenly turn into mudslides; faulting, land subsidence and collapse of underground caverns can swallow houses. Natural and man-made drainage patterns known to ecologists and engineers produce flooding, and beach erosion can wipe out seashore investments.

Popularity and favorable economics in publishing have led metropolitan newspapers to develop Sunday "outlook" or "focus" sections. Editors of these sections offer a good market for analytical, in-depth stories dealing with scientific or medical subjects (178). The pressure to relax network control over prime television hours and to encourage more locally-produced shows may offer the same opportunity for the writer who prefers the broadcast media. Free-lance moviemakers, universities and research-oriented businesses should find new outlets for science material in commercial, educational and cable television.

Apprentice science writers should understand that dealing with other departments, and other specialists in particular, has its perils. Most writers and editors tend to guard their provinces jealously. Having been given the job of handling a special brand of news, they intend to handle it their way. Some fear that the intruder seeks some tiny piece of their territory.

The science writer should first outline the story for the department head. The writer could lose several hours on a story which never makes publication. You may secure approval as casually as having a few quick words at the water cooler or as formally as submitting a story outline with suggestions for pictures. The department head may prefer to contact news sources himself instead of depending on the science writer.

In another situation, the oil editor, the military specialist, the aviation writer or the medical writer may prefer to read the scientific report personally and then make up his mind about whether to develop a story.

When turning over a story to another department, the science writer should recognize three factors:

1. Stories slanted to a special department may grow out of leftover convention papers which are interesting but hardly worthy of a major news story.
2. If the story interests another department, the editor's gratitude may be earned.
3. By lodging such a story with another department a science writer has served part of his function by helping to make the reader aware of what is taking place in science.

Some readers may regard these procedures as devious. The procedures are helpful, however, when the size of the publication, the budget or the professional climate discourages complete specialization. Other readers may regard the suggestions as dealing too much with "applied science" as opposed to "pure science."

Jerry Bishop, science editor of *The Wall Street Journal*, reports that his editors want him to write only stories with economic orientation—applied science. In practice, his applied science stories depend on much pure science information to help the reader understand the new developments (25).

The Third Principle

The third method utilized by science writers to develop science news involves elements of both line and staff positions inside the organization.

Principle 3. Combine science writing with another speciality that will reinforce or feed back on science writing.

The most obvious combination: science and medical writing, where the size of the newspaper or other publications permits. The author's evolution into full-time science writing stemmed from covering aviation and military news. These contain a heavy component of applied scientific and technical knowledge.

As a technique of expanding usefulness, this approach seems promising for the beginning science writer on a small newspaper or magazine. On any publication or wire service the opportunity exists for the writer to initiate stories from his own interests and knowledge. For instance, any general reporter could receive approval for a story dealing with the mob psychology of a race riot. Such a story was done by Earl Ubell and received wide distribution .

It should also be remembered that a weather story explaining the current cold spell or heat wave commands a city editor's attention. New research and development efforts by meteorologists constitute a spectacular scientific attack on a subject of universal interest. Each season offers something.

When one considers the research work of the Weather Bureau, NASA, the U.S. Public Health Service, the Federal Aviation Agency, the Fish and Wildlife Service, the NSF and their state and local counterparts, one can imagine many useful functions for a science-oriented governmental reporter.

Many of the new, emerging specialties have close ties to both the professionals and the material the science writer contacts. Consumer specialists, for example, rely a great deal on scientific test results for objective comparisons of the safety, durability and performance of various products. Environmental subjects require writers to sift through extensive claims and counterclaims, all growing out of research, about the nature of air and water pollution, pesticides, noise and other contaminants.

Politics, particularly the politics of science and technology, cannot be considered as separated from a writer's normal coverage. At one point 50 universities had set up interdisciplinary institutes of science and public policy. These institutes, in turn, organized the Science and Public Policy Studies Group at Massachusetts Institute of Technology as a clearing house for their efforts. And the pressures and divisions of urban life have increased the interest in research performed by the social scientists.

Jerry Bishop of *The Wall Street Journal* has noted how stock-shaking drug developments announced during a scientific meeting can set almost all of the science writers working for the business editors (26:32). *Fortune* magazine regularly reports on scientific developments for its business-oriented readers. As Walter Sullivan, science news editor of *The New York Times,* noted, the technical process of desalting sea water is so intertwined with economics that the two cannot be separated (244:7). The success of the American Telephone and Telegraph Co., as seen by *Time* magazine, hinges on swift application of basic science to communication (20:75).

A natural alliance of interests and high feedback exists for the writer in science and education. One science writer competes with the opposition newspaper's education writer as often as he competes with the science editor. This results from a difference in the way territories are drawn between newspapers. From elementary school through the university level, from the local school district to the national level, school news involves science news. News sources are identical, in many cases, for both types of stories as research mingles evermore with education.

Contraception and nutrition grab so much newspaper space that the woman interested in science writing could begin on the women's section. A very creditable science story was written about food processing research by Betty Stuart Smith, *Christian Science Monitor,* following a visit to the Argonne National Laboratory (226:10).

Some Dead Ends

Some newspaper positions offer little opportunity for developing a "science sideline." Generally the sports department can be a dead end for the science writer. Oceanographic research with immediate application to fishing occurs seldom.

Agriculture writers, however, seem close to much basic research of interest to the general reader and the farmer. Harold M. Schmeck, Jr., became intrigued with proposals of Canada's Department of Agriculture to use computers for pest control (207:128). One interesting paper at the 123rd annual meeting of the British Association for the Advancement of Science proposed "cropping" of wild game for protein (97:20).

Ruth Moore of *The Chicago Sun-Times*, author of popular scientific books, combines science writing with coverage of urban renewal and public welfare (34:44).

Feature writers also appear in a good position to develop proficiency in science reporting.

Applying all these techniques daily would strain the talents of a virtuoso science writer. He would need, in addition, a daily newspaper devoted entirely to science.

Sometimes, as the evening fires burn low, wistful science writers will speculate that such a publication will appear. With the dawn comes reality; although not impossible, such a periodical seems highly improbable. These variations of science writing may help the beginning writer assay the ways in which he will operate. Hopefully he will be stimulated to conceive better ones. Only by demonstrating usefulness to his publication can the science writer earn an unqualified berth.

Science and the Small City Newspaper

The most promising field for applying these techniques lies in smaller city newspapers. A 1964 tabulation of the 200 active and lifetime members of the National Association of Science Writers showed only 11 writing for newspapers of 100,000 circulation or less. Only four members worked for publications of less than 50,000 (23:16).

The study, done by Jules B. Billiard of *The National Geographic*, revealed that 39 were employed by newspapers with circulations of 100,000 to 250,000; 18 on newspapers of 250,000 to 500,000; 12 on papers of 500,000 to 750,000; and 12 on papers circulating more than 750,000 copies a day. In addition, 16 NASW active members wrote for news services or syndicates. Thirty-eight worked for magazines, and the rest classed themselves as primarily free-lancers.

Science writers are well paid, by the standards of journalism. Three-fourths earn more than $10,000 a year (162:11). The studies did not reflect the salary scale of NASW's associate members who are primarily public relations, teaching and government information personnel. The science writers' salaries are the equivalent of those received by the scientists with whom they deal.

All levels of newspapers in the United States lack science -oriented personnel on the news and copy desks, where news is selected and edited.

The statistics lead to these conclusions:

1. The majority of U.S. newspapers, those under 100,000 circulation, employ no one whose interests and training qualify them to write, edit or choose science stories for their local, state or national importance.
2. The financial rewards of science writing make it attractive for the beginner to sharpen his talents on the small and medium newspapers in order to move to the larger publications.

The variety of work assigned a writer on a newspaper of smaller size almost guarantees a rapid education in practical writing, editing and managing a newspaper. However, this also has its pitfalls. The greatest is what Jack Smith, science writer for *The Cincinnati Enquirer,* calls the "warm body syndrome" that afflicts all editors (228:45). The symptoms include an uncontrollable urge to assign any task at hand to the nearest warm, breathing human body.

Carl Heintze describes local coverage this way:

> Science to our editors means different things. It means you talk to the city health department . . . it means you supposedly know something about local medical politics . . . it means you do handout rewrites of the National Science Foundation and the Cancer Society . . . it means that the wire desk will use on Page One that handout which United Press International wrote out of Chicago, even though you know that if you wrote the same story, it would go inside because it was "local" and just a handout.

In many ways it [local science] is harder to write than the big stories which come from the meetings you hear about but seldom get to attend.

It is reducing science and the scientific revolution to its lower common demoninators, explaining the significance of DNA experiments to those more interested in the Giants' standing . . . sorting out the confusion of the thermonuclear bomb to those whose greater problem is disposal of an increasing supply of polluted air and sewage, two other important man-made evils [94:33].

Arthur R. Hill found his work on *The Roanoke Times* (Virginia) interesting, challenging, and varied:

My own beat includes education, science, music criticism, police and courts once a week and general assignment on Sundays, when I am one of two reporters on duty.

Science is a relatively recent addition to *The Times*. . . . It was the desire of a new city editor three years ago to have more medical news of local origin in the paper. I was given the responsibility of developing this area and, in return, the airport was shifted off my beat.

I soon found that the exclusion of all but the medical sciences would not give our readers adequate coverage; in fact, I think reader interest in science has been, and is, ahead of the interest exhibited by many newspapers. The state's largest scientifically oriented college lies squarely in our circulation area; the other is only 2½ hours away by road.

Most of my work is devoted to features. . . . I also have discovered that science is not local in the sense that other newspaper beats are. . . . Attention must be given to developments elsewhere . . . there is no way of predicting when a California scientist may visit the area or stimulate a local experiment. Nor does a science story need to have a local angle, as long as it is interesting . . . *The Times* recently started a weekly science column which, hopefully, will keep our readers and this writer in touch with . . . national developments [96:37].

Two conclusions for science writers in smaller cities follow:

1. Science news is where you find it, and development of such news depends heavily upon the writer.
2. If you intend to write science news, some care should be taken when you pick the newspaper to make sure that there is a news source available and that the newspaper executives have some desire, however slight, to develop these sources.

The town one picks can be critical. For example, the smallest newspaper with a NASW member is *The Post-Bulletin* (circulation 27,000) of Rochester, Minnesota, home of the famous Mayo Clinic. From such a base for operations—no pun intended—other variations are possible.

Cross-Media Communications

News sources and material permit the science writer to engage in free-lance writing or in "cross-media communications," a term preferred by Edward W. Barrett, former dean of the Graduate school of Journalism at Columbia University (17).

The universal appeal of scientific information perhaps makes free-lancing easier for science writers than for generalists. Certainly enough active markets exist which accept the work of science writers to keep many of them busy in their spare time.

Arthur J. Snider of *The Chicago Daily News* contributes the "Progress of Medicine" column to *Science Digest*. Richard Lewis, *Chicago Sun-Times,* wrote for *The Bulletin of the Atomic Scientists* before becoming editor.

Walter Sullivan, *The New York Times,* and Alton Blakeslee, Associated Press, produce books regularly. Often these are syndicated to newspapers when the subject has such universal appeal as how to avoid a heart attack.

The NASW tells beginning writers to land a job on the small or medium-sized daily first, then seek out free-lance assignments (91:3).

Each medium imposes different demands on the science writer, advises Martin Mann, former president of NASW. Rarely do opportunities simply fall into the writer's lap.

"They come to those who seek them and, even more important, are technically equipped to handle them," says Mann (147:2). The NASW operates a Writing Markets Committee to acquaint members with free-lance possibilities.

The NASW also provides the *NASW Clipsheet,* sent to all members. It contains reproductions of science stories contributed by members. In addition to allowing members to compare one another's writing, the *Clipsheet* provides a swift review of news sources and story ideas.

Science specialization also helps the writer advance his career in the mass media. Ian S. Menzies moved successively from science writer to business editor, managing editor and senior editor of *The Boston Globe.* John Troan took over the editorship of *The Pittsburgh Press.* The experience of Howard Simons in writing about science is reflected in *The Washington Post* where he is managing editor. Weldon Wallace of *The Baltimore Sun,* Robert Cowen of *The Christian Science Monitor* and Stuart Loory of *The Herald Tribune* and *The Los Angeles Times* used their science writing experience to advantage in overseas bureaus. Albert Rosenfeld, science and medicine editor for *Life,* moved to *Family Health* as managing editor soon after its founding as a consumer-oriented chronicle of medical and health research.

The Daily Science Newspaper

A daily science newspaper has some practical and much emotional appeal; it also represents considerable financial risk. In 1965-66 the White House Council on Scientific and Technical Information and McGraw-Hill, Inc. cooperated in producing a prototype issue of such a newspaper. Behind the experiment lay several assumptions. One was that daily newspapers cannot provide a volume of news from scientific meetings, details on federal budgets for scientific research, legislative and policy decisions in world-capitals and other science-related matters. Another assumption: Scientists, science-oriented managers, university administrators, businessmen and students would read such a mix. To help close a gap in scientific communications, the publication could have included a daily listing of fresh articles in hundreds of journals, giving individual scientists a running view of their field comparable to that of the daily stock market tables.

In fact, the general aim was to provide a view of the world of science and technology comparable to that presented for business through *The Wall Street Journal.* Of course, this was in the period of rising federal R&D budgets, before they leveled and even shrunk. There were hopes that *Science Daily* would become self-sustaining. Although financing was never projected in detail, the planners hoped to find a basic professional unity among the many disciplines of its potential subscribers. This well-paid, highly-educated audience could have been attractive to advertisers vending scientific equipment, consumer goods and personal services. Average salaries of more than $15,000 annually represented tremendous purchasing power. The project would have tested a great many ideas.

There always has been some question about scientists needing, or even wanting, such a frequent exposure to all fields of science and technology, to science policy and politics or to the literature. Several scientific leaders believe the subjects of science cannot possibly mesh with daily journalism. Others want more empirical evidence.

However, the pilot issue was never tested. The project collapsed on encountering another of those peculiarities of American journalism. Art Kranish, editor and publisher of a Washington-based newsletter *(Science Trends)*, publicized the effort (127). Partly because the federal agency representatives on the Council on Scientific and Technical Information were reluctant to discuss the project in detail, it appeared as an economic threat to *Science Trends* and possibly to other communications media as well. Congressmen and senators asked questions

In the end, thousands of copies of the pilot issue were destroyed. Distribution and readership testing at one or more scientific meetings, including the AAAS, were canceled. The idea, however, has not died. In the 1970s many of the persons connected with the project were approached by the new "communications companies" for their experiences with the pilot. The current trend toward more special interest publications, in contrast to those covering broader audiences, seems promising. But still untested are the basic questions about audience unity and monetary support from advertising and subscription revenue.

Several changes have taken place in the equation. Computerized services have made literature search faster and more current in many fields. Research and development have pulled back from the frantic pace of "big science" that was set during the 1960s. New visual media, including cable television and the film-video cassettes that play through a television set may prove more attractive than a print format. All these leave the daily science newspaper very much a project for the future.

7

Special Problems and Ethics

John Troan, formerly a Washington science writer for the Scripps-Howard Newspapers, can look back on one "scoop" that sums up many of the special problems a science writer faces.

On January 6, 1964, the Public Health Service announced that within five days the press would receive the long-awaited federal report linking smoking and cancer. On January 11, more than 250 reporters would be locked inside the State Department auditorium, handed a 387-page scientific report and given two hours to read and ask questions about this report and its implication. None could file a story until the doors were unlocked.

Release of the information obviously was planned to gain the maximum space in the Sunday newspapers. The release time did not hinge on the completion of the research work or compilation of the report. The time was hardly sufficient to study such a massive report. Troan faced competition, as do most science writers. The subject had high reader interest.

Troan took two actions (214:1). He moved to learn exactly what the official report said, although the scientific and medical facts were generally in the open literature.

He knew none of the committee members well. For him, then, an official leak from one of the committee members was unlikely. Other reporters with better contacts might secure a clandestine briefing or perhaps even a copy of the report. Troan did know several co-workers of the committeemen at various institutions in the country. Nothing resulted from a direct inquiry to these acquaintances about the report's contents. Then he appealed to the scientists' egos. He would say: "But Bill, you don't mean to say that (using the committeeman's name) hasn't told even his *friends* about the report, do you?" Rather than appear out of touch with the developments, the men talked. From these conversations Troan prepared his story.

Then he showed the story to three men who had seen the report. He told these men: "Of course you won't tell me what's in the report, but at least tell what's in my story which is way off base."

These officials, in effect, read and approved the story. Troan's account appeared two days before the report was released—a clear "beat" on the story.

In succession, Troan met and overcame these problems to securing many a science news story:

1. Control over the news by U.S. government officials.
2. Accuracy, fairness and completeness of the story within the constraints of the time and space available.
3. Checking by sources of information qualified to speak on the subject, analyze the scientific data and describe how the official conclusions were reached. Because of the nature of this story, he was unable to give the usual identification of his sources.

In none of his conversations did he fail to identify himself as a newsman seeking a story. He did not deceive his sources by publishing a story from information accepted as confidential and off the record. In return, his sources showed respect for accuracy and his pledge that both the information and the check for accuracy would be accepted on a "not-for-attribution" basis.

Before the story was distributed for publication, it passed the usual tests for criminal and civil libel, including malice and possible damage to the reputations of individuals and corporations.

Every science story must respect accuracy in presenting a scientist's results. Although no case could be found in which a scientist sued a newspaper on the precise grounds that his reputation as a scientist had been damaged by inaccurate reporting, a real possibility exists for such a lawsuit. Writers must remember that prompt correction of an error and truth of the printed material remain the only effective responses outside the courts. If the matter goes to court, either correction or truth may become the only legal defense.

Laws regarding invasion of privacy apply to writers of science stories as well as to writers of other material. Generally, a reporter may ask any question he desires, seek any favor he wishes or request any material or poses for photographs that occur to him at an interview. The person being interviewed then must decide exactly how much cooperation he gives the writer. "Answer questions fully, but don't feel that you have to bare your soul. . . . Don't make statements you don't want quoted," bluntly advises a company that employs many scientists (215:8).

Most disputes between scientists and writers are resolved with a good feeling before an interview ends. This writer knows of no instance in which a science reporter deliberately set out to make a scientist appear foolish. On the other hand, both the scientist and the reporter face some close and tough decisions:

1. When the scientist speaks as a professional researcher and also as official adviser or member of the government.
2. When his individual research is financed by public monies, a private foundation or a company that hopes for financial gain from his research. As mentioned, the scientist usually remains the best judge of when his material is ready for public presentation.
3. When security regulations or the terms of his grant require a scientist to get permission before discussing his research.

4. When the scientist works for a company whose financial future depends on the ability of its employees to protect classified information under federal contracts.
5. When the research involves discoveries or processes that the scientist's industrial employer intends to patent or utilize to gain economic advantage in business competition.

When the complexities of many scientific topics are considered in addition to these restrictions, little wonder that interviews may begin nervously. Little wonder also that science writers are reluctant to dictate notes to a rewrite man or attempt to organize raw notes and dictate "from the top of their head" without writing and rechecking a story.

Often the organization or scientist involved will correct errors when the error was not directly the reporter's fault. The Population Reference Bureau found itself in this position when a typographical error added 50 million people to the bureau's estimate for the year 2010.

Opportunities to libel come more often than expected. For instance, the NASA Manned Spacecraft Center in 1963 issued a statement labeling one of its employees a thief (149). Although the announcement of the man's suspension was prepared with the knowledge of responsible center officials, the press announcement gave no source for the allegations. In addition, a correction had been penciled on the announcement to alter the estimated amount. No reporter would write a story from such an announcement. This kind of story goes to the police or courthouse reporter for legal verification of the arrest and charge.

Science writers also should be aware of "anti-science" bias that develops from the increased impact of science and technology. On the newspaper staff this may seem to reflect itself in slaps in print aimed at science or scientists. For example, a recent headline declared, "Obscenity OK If It's Science," although the story indentified the person writing several objectional letters only as an author seeking book material on "sexual misbehavior in modern suburbia" (174:1). Nothing in the story indicated any systematic research project by an individual representing himself as a scientist.

These small things should be viewed with tolerance, just as one would regard such statements as this from astronaut Frank Borman: "A properly trained pilot is probably the best scientific observer in captivity" (33:15). Less amusing, however, are fawning, overwrought stories occasionally found about some allegedly scientific cosmetic or medical products. For example, the author's file has an account of some "cosmetic silicone injection therapy" purporting to remove wrinkles, increase tolerance to sunlight and improve the morale of aging women. It sounds as if the author got her treatment free.

Science writers will find their fellows have some definite opinions on how the world and newspapers should be run from a so-called scientific viewpoint. Watson Davis, for instance, has stated these hard-and-fast policies to which he would commit science writers:

1. Horoscopes should not be published . . . propaganda for the superstition of astrology.
2. Cigarette smoking and habitual use of alcohol should be discouraged . . . the dangers of these common practices get little or no time, much less equal time, on television.
3. Medical nostrums, food fads, and dangerous and useless cosmetics should be campaigned against . . . some newspapers and magazines still take drug advertisements almost as bad as those for patent medicines.
4. The lack of public protection against diseases that can be prevented by immunization should be protested and the situation brought to the attention of readers, public health officials and doctors.
5. Anti-vivisection propaganda should be resisted as a barrier to essential medical research . . . born of sentimentality (by those) who seemingly love dogs and cats more than babies or fellow human beings.
6. Fluoridation of public water supplies should be supported . . . .disgraceful and amazing feat in local elections of the adding of minute amounts of harmless fluoride compounds to

drinking water to cause teeth to have fewer cavities . . . mass media should dispel the lack of knowledge that prevents this useful procedure.

7. Support of extreme measures seemingly based on scientific findings should be avoided . . . mass media should not take a supporting stand in banning insecticides, favoring . . . so-called natural fertilizers . . . medical treatments of an undisclosed or unauthenticated nature, etc.

8. Birth control should be upheld as personal privilege and a needed world population policy.

9. The public should be made aware of the methods and techniques of education, persuasion, and decision . . . about which not enough is known, and mass media controllers should take leadership for discovery and application.

10. Prevention of war . . . a problem that is unresolved and one that is worthy of major attention for discussion and informative reporting.

11. Freedom of religion . . . because of the past conflicts of science and religion . . . the mass media should be concerned with fulfilling the traditional American freedoms of press, speech, and religion [64:15].

This "platform" illustrates that even experienced science writers can slip into the belief that science can arbitrate a host of political and social issues. Advises Dr. Polykarp Kusch, physicist and Nobel laureate:

Science cannot do a very large number of things, and to assume that science may find a technical solution to all problems is the road to disaster. . . . Science, in itself, is not the source of the ethical standards, the moral insight, the wisdom that is needed to make value judgments, though it is an important ingredient in making of value judgments. . . . An appalling number of citizens believe that it is up to the scientist to make the judgment, as though he had an especially valid set of values. . . . A more temperate view of this authority of science is necessary [133:3].

Studies have convinced Dr. Hillier Krieghbaum that the result of a science story may depend on how readers convert accurate and unbiased reporting to fit their own prejudices and biases or on the way science news is packaged. "Scientists should consider this finding before they object too vigorously to the way writers have handled news that the scientists wanted to be sure the public would receive," said Dr. Kreighbaum (129:1094).

Gilbert Cant, medical writer, says that he could write a story saying a drug *would not* cure cancer, but somewhere, someone would demand that their doctor supply them with "that new cancer cure" (59:63).

Dr. J.H. Westbrook of the General Electric Laboratory says another uncertainty is that science itself is subject to fads, changes in fashions and the changing interest of scientists and that there is no means of appraising work performed but not published.

Application of a few simple scientific principles will help the layman (and science writer) to avoid errors, says Dr. Joel Hildebrand (95:31). These principles include:

1. Be skeptical of sense impressions; experiments measuring the "brightness" of "really clean teeth" are too rough for more than general measurements.
2. Remember that every well-planned experiment is a question put to nature and that the experiment is colored by the form of the question.
3. Be alert to the fact that scientists, like other people, show a vast capacity to believe the incredible in people and are influenced thereby.
4. Beware the left-handed flattery shown science by eagerness to accept pseudo-science.
5. Recognize that scientists believe there is some logical order in the most complex situations.
6. Do not mistake analogy for evidence; to say that the cell is to the body what a man is to society is a clever way to suggest a new idea, but the situations are not parallel.

7. Understand that "laws of nature" describe behavior and do not cause behavior; if nature does not follow the description, the law must be revised.
8. Understand that scientists operate in a world in which general behavior is predictable but the individual event cannot be identified.
9. Note that the more significant, definite and widely applicable is any discovery, the more concisely and clearly it can be stated.

There are "gray" areas in science. New ideas, such as a virus-cancer relationship, may take time to be accepted. Writers have no rules—only guides here.

Nate Haseltine, medical writer for *The Washington Post*, suggested "Reporters should damp down everything a scientist tells you. Handle it with a grain of salt" (92).

Ethics in Science Writing

Persons as diverse as Albert Einstein and Cosmonaut Yuri Gagarin have complained about treatment by the press. "The German press has reproduced a deliberately distorted version of my words, as indeed was only to be expected with the press muzzled as it is today," said Dr. Einstein in the early days of Hitler's Germany (71:207). His statement stands as a reminder for science writers of their need, also, to defend the guarantees of freedom of the press to gather and to publish the facts.

Yet limited freedom can be abused. In Russia, nearly 30 years after Einstein left Germany, Cosmonaut Gagarin's apartment was raided by reporters who rifled his home for family photographs and other memorabilia. "I guess you have pilfered everything," Gagarin told the reporters (217:95).

In the United States in 1960, the National Association of Science Writers attacked an alarming trend. This trend was the offer of magazine advertisers to pay science writers for what amounted to an endorsement of a disinfectant. The writer was identified with his by-line and as a medical news writer for a major metropolitan daily. Members of the NASW approved these two resolutions:

1. A science writer shall take all necessary measures to insure that the information he purveys to the public is accurate, truthful and impartial.
2. A science writer should not for any remuneration by a commercial organization permit his name to be used to promote a commercial service, a commercial product, or a commercial organization. Such activity shall be considered prejudicial to the best interest of this association [57:11].

The word "promote" was chosen above "write." "A writer could lend his name to promote a cause without himself writing a word of copy," said Victor Cohn (57:12), chairman of the revisions committee. The NASW opposes any members signing an ad couched in the form of an article or acceptance of covert payment for mentioning or praising a product in an article or news story. Member writers are forbidden to make and sell reprints of articles which mention any firm favorably. If the publication permits a firm to reproduce an article as an advertisement, the author may not accept payment from the advertiser. The resolution forbids any science writer from producing pamphlets, under his name, praising a commercial cause or product. These restrictions apply to radio and television and printed material.

Science writers may accept commissions to write and produce unsigned pamphlets or advertising copy. They may endorse non-profit causes. On both points, however, other science writers dissent; they believe any payment to a writer should come only from his editor. These writers refuse all other obligations.

The resolution was not aimed at associate members or publicists who openly support causes and products. It applies to the writer who purports to represent the public's interest.

Mention of products is not forbidden. "It can be legitimate news to say that product is good if the writer is being paid only by the editor," said Cohn's report.

Pay, in Cohn's estimate, means any remuneration beyond a drink, a dinner or a bottle of Christmas whisky. Watson Davis, in an article titled "Hucksters in the Temple" (65:17), stood against these favors. "Press conferences and cocktail parties are devices adopted for obtaining scientific publicity," said Davis. So are gifts of liquor and junkets. Davis also feels that a press release date constitutes a threat to force the writer or editor to pay unusual attention for fear that the competition will use the story first.

Science writers, like all reporters, should not misquote, misstate or mislead; their reputation as a writer and reporter is at stake, advises Troan (258:1193). In a literate world, the writer courts professional disaster by reverting to overly sensationalized sex-science writing.

Steven M. Spencer, award-winning medical journalist, cautions against raising false hopes through new medical treatments. "I never write about anything unless several authorities agree it's a significant development (51). This is no light responsibility. Dr. Roger O. Egeberg, the federal assistant secretary for health and scientific affairs in the Department of Health, Education and Welfare, has told doctors they are entering an era when patients are better informed about many medical and health conditions than ever before (208).

Much of this acquisition of knowledge has self-protection as its motive force. Disclosures of the sometimes fatal side effects of drugs during the past decade contributed more to this felt need than the medical profession admits. In the aftermath of federal hearings on the effects of birth control pills, Judith Randal of *The Washington Star* faulted doctors heavily for neglecting to warn patients regularly that no drug exists that is unconditionally safe (195).

Dr. Joseph F. Montague is a physician, medical editor and author of a popular medical advice column. He has warned writers to beware of becoming publicity agents for drug manufacturers (157). He also cautioned against loss of objectivity and sensationalized attack upon doctors and drug makers for the sake of book or publication sales. The closer relationship between science-medical writers and health professionals imposes a new responsibility and relationship, Dr. Irvine H. Page argues (181).

The new relationship bothers science writers also. Mildred Spencer, as NASW president, fretted over the ease with which scientists can speak or call a reporter about a story. In other times, "the science writer went forth to interview his quarry after hearing about his work from other scientists or a professional publication. He knew that there was a story there, a story that had some merit in scientific eyes." Charles Marwick of *Medical World News* acknowledges the risk of being duped by an occasional "operator" or crackpot, but the writer can check other sources on the man's reputation, prior publications in reputable journals and the rationality of the proposals. When Barbara Seaman came under criticism from a drug company public relations man, she was able to show that the point of view expressed in her book about birth control pills coincided with that of several doctors and medical journals; the book also had the approval of a respected director of a medical school's birth control clinic (218).

Responsibility rests no less lightly upon public relations men caught up in events of science. How Spyros Andreopoulous of the Stanford Medical Center's news bureau coped with the first synthesis of DNA and the first American heart transplant has become a classic case study of scientific press activity (9).

Science writers should not develop a defensive attitude toward critics. Dr. Arthur Winter, physician and husband of science writer Ruth Winter of the *Newark New Jersey Star Ledger,* is one of several doctors who has benefited from hearing first about new drugs or procedures from science writers. "I know that science writers can be given information, and that they will report that information accurately and tactfully if properly informed" (278).

Prudence requires the writer to recheck his story when there has been a long delay in publication. After hundreds of thousands of people had read a long-delayed story about a chemical beauty treatment. Connecticut officials raided the clinic, found that the supervising physican had resigned and charged the remaining staff with unlicensed operation of a hospital and practicing medicine without a license (49:67).

In the field of "miracle cures," writers must remain wary of "secret" ingredients that researchers and inventors refuse to disclose. The ethical codes of scientists and doctors require them to submit complete data on such treatments to their colleagues for examination. No ingredients can be withheld from the medical and scientific literature.

Control by Others

Many of the professional practices of the science and medical reporter are controlled by the ethical codes of others. Because the reporter needs the cooperation of scientists and doctors, he must consider their standards. He cannot responsibly jeopardize the professional standing of a news source.

This can become an acute problem when dealing with medical doctors who must remain in good standing with medical associations. Codes adopted by society members are enforced by threat of expulsion from the society. Harris County, Texas, doctors cannot "seek publicity" under the code; the application of this constraint forbids doctors from mention in all newspaper stories and from listing their specialty in telephone books. William P. Steven, former editor of *The Houston Chronicle*, has raised the question that failure to list specialities may jeopardize the health of newcomers to a city when they have no knowledge of local doctors (59:28).

Steven's experience with formulating "codes" for doctor-press relations has been bad. He has found the codes almost always become the vehicle by which doctors attempt to close off all sources of information rather than open up new avenues.

Says Victor Cohn:

We newsmen have learned that what starts as "ethics" can soon become gag rule. Too many local medical societies still make "ethics," much of which has nothing to do with truly ethical behavior, a fetish, and the result in every case is unnecessary bitterness between doctors and the press [53:752].

Great variation exists across the country in these codes. Most have five points in common where the patient and the press are concerned, according to a *Medical Economics* survey by William Bender, Jr. (21:137).

With consent of the patient or his family, most codes permit physicians to tell the press:

1. The patient's name, age and address.
2. The general nature of his illness.
3. The seriousness of his condition: good, fair, poor or critical.
4. The time of the patient's birth or death, when this information is applicable.
5. Any further scientific information that will lead to a better understanding of the progress of medical science where the case involves unusual injury, illness or treatment.

Stories of interest to the science and medical reporters usually fall under Article Five.

"Some medical society rules are more stringent than these. Many are considerably more liberal," Bender stated. He also listed some other guidelines doctors may apply in their relations with reporters, particularly on cases involving violence.

1. In fairness to the reporter, the doctor should ask the patient's permission to talk about the injury. If permission is refused, the doctor should tell the reporter he tried to secure permission. Permission should be sought in a positive manner, without influencing the patient to refuse by the tone or wording.
2. Doctors may attempt to make sure that the patient is newsworthy, although normally the only necessary proof is the fact that the reporter has asked about the patient.
3. Descriptions of injuries or conditions should be translated into nonclinical terms; "penetrating wound" is preferred over "he was knifed."
4. Questions about the cause or motivation of accident victims should be referred to the police, fire department or other public agency having an interest.

5. Rape, intoxication and moral turpitude are difficult to prove, and physicians must resist efforts of the reporter to put words into the doctor's mouth.

6. Doctors should speak only of those things they know of their own observation and not discuss anything told them by reporters, policemen or patients.

Hospital Codes

Hospitals, like the doctor and the writer, deal with information about patients in a manner somewhat prescribed by the local medical societies. Hospital codes generally must be acceptable to the doctors who use the hospital and serve on hospital board and committees. Great variations are found in each city and between private hospitals and public-supported hospitals. By their nature, special hospitals for the alcoholic or mentally disturbed will regard patient information differently from general hospitals. Reporters of medical news should become familiar with local codes.

Large hospitals usually assign persons to handle press inquiries. Medical writers normally work with these public relations officials with little difficulty. General reporters facing constant deadlines encounter more problems. Medical writers also get their share of emergency stories, including those involving police cases, because of their knowledge of hospital personnel.

Emergency or violence cases often develop when a regular press officer in not on duty. This throws the handling of press relations on harried personnel in the emergency room. Because emergency room personnel change around the clock, not all of them are sure what information can be released freely.

The NASW Newsletter has reproduced the code used by the Fairfax County Hospital, Virginia (101:31), as worth studying for several reasons. This code, posted throughout the hospital, specifies in detail who may release news about patients, the information which may be given without the patient's consent and the photography ground rules.

So much variation was found among several hospital codes studied by this author that the best advice is to learn the individual policies of each institute. One hospital, for example, refers reporters to the patient's doctor for all information. At the same time one can receive a full condition report from the admissions desk if one identifies himself as a friend of the family.

The Publishing Rules

Scientist: "You science writers live off the crumbs from our table."

Writer: "Unfortunately, sir, it is a hard life because the crumbs are so often stale."

The rejoinder, attributed to William L. Laurence of *The New York Times* (215:4), sums up one aspect of the science writer-scientist relationship. Science news writers want results immediately, but scientists spend days, weeks, even months studying their data. Then they present the findings first to scientific colleagues in a journal or at an annual meeting. This normally causes little friction because science writers and scientists have adjusted to it.

Some variations have been worked out for scientific information containing high public interest. The NSF used one of these techniques to get the results of a Project Stratoscope flight to the public press. The NSF press release (238) was timed for Sunday newspapers, June 28, 1964. Saturday afternoon Stratoscope's chief scientist, Prof. Martin Schwarzschild, presented the results of his six-month flight analysis to the American Astronomical Society in Phoenix, Arizona. The release was sent to science writers far enough in advance to give them time to secure interviews, comments and background on the importance of the telescope's findings.

Before the limited nuclear test ban became effective, there was intense interest in how the fallout from bomb tests entered the human food chain and how radioactive particles were distributed in the body. The results of a government study on the matter were reserved for the first publication in *Science,* weekly organ of the American Association for the Advancement of Science. This was vigorously protested by several newspapers whose editors and writers believed the research was so important that the public should have been informed first.

Dr. Dael Wolfe, executive officer of the AAAS, defended the priority of scientific publication in an editorial entitled "Author's Choice." Said he:

> The research worker has a choice. If he presents his material in an open meeting or gives it directly to the press, newspapers can report it immediately. The material reaches the public quickly—if at all—but relatively unscreened and rarely in sufficient detail to enable other scientists to form their own judgments about the adequacy of the conclusions. If the report is published in a scientific journal, it does not reach the public as quickly, but when it does, it has survived critical scientific review, has frequently been made clearer as a result of suggestions from the editor or referee, and is published in sufficient detail to enable scientific colleagues to appraise data and methods as well as conclusions.
>
> Custom dictates that the choice be made by the scientists rather than by the institution that supported the work or the editor to whom the account of it is submitted [281:1247].

Two journals of the American Institute of Physics took similar stands. "Scientific discoveries are not the proper material for newspaper scoops," said *Physical Review Letters* (87:5). Editorialized *Applied Physics Letters* (62:3), "Work described elsewhere, prior to scheduled publication in APL will not be considered eligible for publication."

In spite of these strong stands, Robert C. Toth of *The Los Angeles Times* won part of his battle against the use of simultaneous releases on NASA projects high in public interest. One concession was an agreement to publish in *Science* because of the short time-lag between deadline and publication; reports received on a Tuesday can appear on Friday. The other concession was to release material to the press upon *acceptance* for *Science* publication. Another concession was NASA's agreement that on results from such great technological accomplishments as the first Ranger photographs of the moon, NASA would make no attempt to hold the results for the journals. In recounting his conflict with NASA, Toth commented (257:17): "I guess we've gotten something of a victory, if it holds up. Now we've got to work on the other agencies."

Dr. Philip Abelson, editor of *Science*, has expressed these thoughts:

> I feel that newspapers and scientific journals are not in serious competition with each other. These media are worlds apart in audience, coverage, and precision of technical detail [2:5].

Dr. Abelson sympathized with the AIP stand but felt that it was too rigid. Likely this conflict will last as long as there are scientists and writers.

Credit Where Due

Scientists should receive credit, even in science stories, for facts and ideas they present. Most science writers seem conscientious about this. In examining more than 2,000 science stories, only one serious credit omission was found.

In February, 1964, an article appeared in *The Sciences,* published by the New York Academy of Sciences, titled "Science in the Kitchen" (212:6) and credited to Dr. G.D. Brown and *The New Scientist.* The story described the scientific processes taking place when food is cooked, protected from oxidation, "buffered" to control hydrolysis by acidity and given some psychological improvements by the chef. In May, 1964, a strikingly similar article appeared under the by-line of a physician who writes a medical column (270:24). The wording and sequence of topics were identical in many cases to that used in *The Sciences* but without credit.

This does not imply that a long series of credits must clutter each story. When using a journal article as the starting point for a personal or telephone interview, a reporter will likely gain enough new, fresh material that journal credit is no longer needed. For the benefit of scientific readers, as well as a verification of the authenticity of the data, even interview articles often mention that the scientist has published the material in a reputable journal.

For *The Saturday Review* of July 4, 1964 (136:38), science editor John Lear produced an article dealing with the explosion of a giant star on that same day in the year 1054. Blair Justice of *The Houston Post* reworked the information, looked up other detail from reference works and added material from an interview with a scientist (120:2). In the end, Justice's story bore little resemblance to the source of his story idea.

Humor and Science

"Science is so damn dull. Why don't you ever write a funny story about science?"

This is one of the most common complaints science writers receive from deskmen. Few "fun" stories appear on the science beat. There is no way to guide the beginner to any mother lode of scientific humor. Nor can one tell anyone how to write amusingly about science.

Dr. James R. Newman has questioned whether or not scientific humor is even possible:

There is no obvious reason why it should be; the substance of science, ranging from acoustics to zymurgy, is scarcely designed to make laughter hold its sides [173:243].

He concluded that gentle ridicule, inside jokes and satire that punctures the phony weightiness of any profession is healthy, but it hardly forces you to laugh in spite of oneself. Language of science is one barrier to crackling humor.

Dan Greenberg often uses his fictional character "Dr. Grant Swinger" to parody the maneuvers of scientists and administrators to obtain research grants from foundations and government. Occasionally scientists themselves unbend. The humor of the situation was not lost on Dr. David E.H. Jones in describing his attempts to build an unridable bicycle (115) in a serious effort to find out why bicycles are so stable that only a few people fail to master them. And writers translating his research into popular press stories did not have to strain for their humor (138).

In *Nature*, a prim journal, an anonymous scientist told of collecting his beard shavings daily and weighing them carefully. He was curious about his beard's erratic growth. When he was alone in his island laboratory, with no immediate journey planned back to civilization, his harvest was light. However, the growth achieved "unusually high rates," he said, as the time neared for his returns to the mainland and feminine companionship.

Two other scientists, with a fey turn of mind and tongue in cheek, hunted for earthly comparisons for their measured densities of moon rocks. Not content with comparing densities by transmitting sound waves through comparable earth rocks, they expanded to other materials. In *Science* they reported similarities between the lunar rocks and aged cheeses (211), "which leads us to suspect that perhaps old hypotheses are best, after all, and should not be lightly discarded." Their experiment produced an amusing story for Stuart Auerbach (15).

Alexander Dorozynski, a free-lance science writer, kept his science clean, although light-hearted, in a whimsical article berating himself for his difficulty in understanding the theories of relativity (67:14). His slightly irreverent article produced no protests.

Newspaper writers often embrace the temptation to attempt humor based on exotic and esoteric titles of research projects and papers. Such attempts are "cornball" and "bad form" in the eyes of most science writers.

Scientists do not appreciate the humor. In addition, the generality of the title may obscure worthwhile and even interesting research. Congressman Charles A. Mosher, a former Ohio editor, reads many such titles as a member of the House of Representatives committee on science and astronautics. In a broadcast to his constituents he counterpunched one "funny" story based on project titles in this way:

> It's so easy to make a popular news headline by poking fun at some of the activities of research scientists. Some politicians frequently use this cheap way to get their names before the public . . . and there also is a type of shallow, superficial news reporting and editorial writing along those same lines. It's so easy for a lazy reporter to just take a list of the titles . . . and make a funny news item . . . as if in horror that the taxpayers' money would be squandered on such seeming nonsense. . . . There are hundreds of examples . . . think twice before you too easily heap scorn and ridicule on scientific research which superficially may seem silly to your practical mind [159:3].

The *NASW Newsletter* (240:31) reprinted several popularized descriptions compiled by Carl W. Larsen, a Nieman Fellow and staff member of the University of Chicago.

1. "The Oral Health of Icelandic Peoples": Part of a larger study on how different foods, climates and customs affect the incidence of painful mouth diseases.
2. "Studies in Silent Thinking": Study in the thought processes of mentally disturbed persons, particularly schizophrenics, who often refuse to talk; this makes communication and treatment difficult because the patient is unwilling or unable to say what he thinks or feels.
3. "Red Tuna and Yellow Fat Diseases in the Cat": An investigation related to reducing the amounts of fatty acids in the human blood stream. Fish oils contain desirable, unsaturated fatty acids but also produce a toxic effect in cats—and possibly other mammals—called yellow fat disease.
4. "A Stereotactic Atlas of the Beagle Brain": Dogs, in this case Beagles, are the most suitable animals to use for experimenting with surgical treatment for many nerve disor-

ders. Before doctors can attempt some of these treatments on dogs, they need to know the function of every part of the dog's brain with extreme accuracy in order to insert probes or other instruments.

It is well for the science writer to be alert for frivolous and wasteful research or duplication. However he needs to know more than the title of the project. The scientific professions also might spare themselves grief by more understandable titles or abstracts.

Magazine writer David O. Woodbury considers himself expert in blending science and humor (282:22). He keeps watch for amusing anecdotes and experiences of scientists and writers thrown into contact with strange equipment, unusual medical situations and the do-it-yourself science projects. Woodbury makes himself the butt of the humor in many cases.

Dorozynski achieved humor in his account of battling through the medical, scientific and political bureaucracy to get an interview with Soviet physicist Lev Landau, a Nobel Prize winner (68:25).

Humor possibilities exist in the deluge of scientific toys and kits now on sale. In a more serious vein, parents and children may welcome guidance on the type, quality and usefulness of these products. If the writer does not feel qualified to evaluate them himself, a scientist with children might do the job in an interview.

The subject matter and the situations of science and medicine appear to offer an opportunity for the humorist. When he has to strain to get the punch line out of the typewriter, he probably has crossed the very narrow line between humor and offensiveness.

Sensationalism and Fairness

Sensationalism likely can never be entirely removed from science journalism. Both scientists and writers seem to agree on extreme examples of sensational science writing. Some scientists probably will never be satisfied with anything less formal than the technical journal account. However, as has been mentioned, Ubell's experience with some "jazzing up" of science copy indicates that milder degrees of "sensationalizing" improve readership among scientists as well as nonscientists.

The "extreme" examples occur seldom. The story that one scientist or writer considers sensational may appear to others as a respectable attempt to popularize a scientific report. All shades of "sensationalism" have been found.

Sensational treatment brought *The Houston Chronicle* a bitter protest from a doctor. The story involved an attempt to see if a connection existed between intelligence and fertility in women. (Some subjects naturally lend themsleves to flashy treatment; sex and any hint of a bosom versus brains conflict is one of these.) The doctor's scientific paper appeared in the journal of his specialty (237:297-301).

At the direction of the city editor, a writer renowned for his colorful stories obtained a copy of the journal. He prepared a Sunday story that invoked images of brainless beauties and bustless Phi Beta Kappas (188:1). The story theme accurately followed the journal paper; extensive quotes were used from the journal. Missing, however, was the physician's conclusion that three-fourths of the female population were mixtures of these physical-mental types.

The Chronicle's Bureau of Accuracy and Fair Play sent a clipping to the doctor for comment. Here is a key quotation from his reply:

> Your quotations of my classifications of women were correct, but you left out the important statement in the beginning of the paper which was stressed again in the summary that the pure types are in the minority and that more women are mixtures. Instead of that you took a small observation from the last pages out of context and made it the leading issue of the entire report with a sensational headline. This gives the impression as if there are only two kinds of women, the ones with flat chests and brains and the ones with large breasts and low I.Q.'s. This misrepresenta-

tion created an understandably violent protest from all over the world as if I did not know that there are many women who have both good intelligence and good physical endowments and that fortunately the well-balanced females are in the majority.

In order to dramatize the "bust-or-brains" slogan you added pictures and interviews with bosomy movie stars to your articles. The comments of these ladies, based on distorted information, made my investigation a joke [236:1-4].

One straightforward sentence would have clarified accurately that most women fall somewhere between the two extremes. Each scientific paper generally has the researcher's conclusion stated plainly. If this position is stated, any accusations of sensationalism must be moderated by this evidence that the writer made a genuine effort to convey this position. No amount of hyperactive writing can wipe out such a sentence or a paragraph.

Such callous and sometimes hypocritical treatment in sexual matters can damage research. Recognizing this, many science and medical writers have risked losing their chance to be "first" with stories. A very good example of this deals with the landmark work of Dr. William Howard Masters and Virginia E. Johnson. Many writers knew they were using human subjects in studying human sexual response under laboratory conditions. Their progress was recorded in medical literature, and writers could have relied on this for their story. Respecting the pleas of the researchers, the writers waited until the appearance of the Masters-Johnson books before reporting on the easily-sensationalized work.

Newspaper writers cherish the axiom that two sides exist for every question and try to present both. Sometimes they fail to recognize both sides in scientific or medical research. Writers for *The New York Times* and *The Wall Street Journal* demonstrated their alertness and fairness in September, 1964, when science writers received a newsletter from an association of prominent doctors urging studies of artificial sweeteners as possible cancer-causing agents. The sources were qualified, respected, authoritative. A story could have been written from the doctors' point of view. However, both *The New York Times* (52:30) and *The Wall Street Journal* (180:6) printed additional statements about the chemicals from a standard medical index, from Food and Drug Administration officials and from companies manufacturing artificial sweeteners.

On other occasions the science writer and his editors may need iron-clad constitutions to print the results of checking other scientists about a report. Earl Ubel tells of printing the unsweetened reactions of several scientists to reports of another man's scientific findings. "He's no longer speaking to me," said Ubell (261:6).

These problems of science writing have only inexact solutions. By negotiation with scientists, the writer can minimize the restrictions. His best tools are knowledge of the subject, ground rules of the professions and initiative.

Accuracy and fairness should remain the overriding qualities of any story. As illustrated by Troan's cancer-smoking story, writers may find that often they return to old news sources for extraordinary new favors.

8
Science
and Censorship

Access to information is the key to all reporting. From Sparta, 500 B.C., until the present, governments of all varieties have attempted to control what people see, hear or read (90:1304). The increasing power of the government purse in scientific research brings the subject deeply into the realm of public concern. At the same time, this increased public support at all levels of government engages public officials in a process that formerly was fairly private, self-policing and self-regulating.

The right of a free press is guaranteed in the First Amendment of The Constitution. However, the freedom to publish is not absolute, often being suspended during wartime. Nor is this freedom automatically recognized, as William Hines of *The Washington Star* discovered when he was invited to dispatch a story over a new communications satellite in 1960. For transmission, Hines wrote: "It was a stunt, of course. A gimmick. But there was an aura of history about it that made participation in the stunt impossible to resist."

The paragraph emerged from outer space reading: "This historical experiment may well be the forerunner of tomorrow's mode of communication."

Army officials apologized following a protest by Hines and other newsmen to the House of Representatives Committe on Government Information. The Army Office of Information said the change was made by a Signal Corps technician and that "the authority to change matters of fact appears to have been misapplied" (108:34). For many writers this was the first realization that any authority existed to change matters of fact.

Members of the National Association of Science Writers at their annual meeting in December, 1963, filed an official protest against information policies of NASA (232:5). The principal NASW complaint was NASA's refusal to discuss public information policies with NASW representatives.

A few years later, in 1970, the science writers were quarreling with the AAAS about being left out of business sessions. At a time when protest groups were trying to force changes on the AAAS, writers who were official delegates to the sessions obtained a competitive edge over those left out. Although some groups, including the American Medical Association and the American Psychological Association, admit writers to even their intramural policy debates, many do not. One day of the annual meeting of the National Academy of Sciences, for example, is closed to the press. Wil Lepkowski of McGraw-Hill World News found this little handicap to learning how the NAS president proposed to reorganize the academy and the National Research Council. He quizzed members of a sister group, the National Academy of Engineering, about the proposed reorganization and found it was rejected by the academy membership.

Victor Cohn has reported some universities require writers to get "administrative clearance" before interviewing scientists to talk. "Some government-employed scientists and technical men are afraid to say 'Hello' on the telephone without asking you to 'go-through' information officer go-between," he says.

This chapter discusses some ways government officials attempt to control access to information. In 1966 Congress enacted what is known as the Freedom of Information Act. It opened many records and reports previously closed by administrative rulings.

Guidelines issued by the attorney general outlined 3 reasons for keeping some records closed and ways to appeal a refusal to give writers access to disputed material. The law also gave citizens the right to sue federal officials to open avenues of access; this right has been used more often by business and by consumer advocates than by the press. (Materials on the law and its meaning can be obtained from the Freedom of Information Center, University of Missouri School of Journalism, Columbia, Missouri, 65201.)

Refusal to disclose official actions is not limited to federal officials. State, county and city officials act in similar ways when the information may embarass them and their bosses or may open controversies. The tolerance of public officials for the people who elect them and pay their expenses often appears very low. But there is an essential difference in the actions of a private and a public individual; in the public sector, the writer constantly meets practices designed to frustrate the right to know what its officials are doing with tax money.

Cohn urges reporters to dig deeper into the effects of new discoveries and gadgetries upon people and public policy. "This means poking our noses into more government agencies," he says.

> The Washington press corps, naturally, must take the lead in scrutinizing federal science agencies. But the same challenges face science and medical writers in every city and state. Our local agencies and local medical societies (which often act, in effect, as quasigovernment agencies) are far too little watched [53:753].

Evidence that pressure from newsmen exerts an influence for freedom may be found in Earl Ubell's report on the effectiveness of a joint committee of the NASW and the American Society of Newspaper Editors (264:12) in securing certain types of information about manned space flight that previously had been denied newsmen by NASA.

Robert C. Toth found the information dispensed through NASA improved in both accuracy and volume during the 1963-65 period. Credit for this improvement should go to Julian Scheer, a former North Carolina newsman, whose performance in the agency information post earned the confidence of NASA's top administrators, said Toth (256).

The act that established the National Aeronautics and Space Administration permits witholding information from the press for only two reasons: (a) information authorized or required by federal statue to be withheld and (b) information classified to protect the national security (165:14). This regulation obliges NASA to respect security imposed by divison of the Department of Defense, the Atomic Energy Commission and the Department of State.

Security considerations are strong when NASA space launchings use military rockets. Conversely, the rockets and spaceships developed by NASA carry certain security priorities where the military, particularly the Air Force, sees potential defense applications.

No such national security requirement covers the National Institutes of Health, research divisions of the Department of Health, Education and Welfare. Here are some of the problems Stuart Loory reported in getting a story at the NIH:

> The truth is that officials in some parts of the National Institutes of Health too often act like they're guarding secrets too delicate for even the Atomic Energy Commission or the Department of Defense. That's why it took me two months to do a story on a National Institute of Allergy and Infectious Diseases program to develop vaccines against respiratory diseases. With a modicum of cooperation, the story could have been done in a week and would have reflected far more credit on NIAID than it eventually did [144:28].

Loory encountered almost all of the roadblocks that can be thrown in the way of a reporter. "Security" was never mentioned. His hunt began promisingly "with a box in the NIH house organ last fall calling for volunteers with young, virile colds who would be paid for submitting to blood tests and throat swabs."

Usually when an agency goes into more or less public print, its officers are ready to discuss the matter. "My zeal in pursuing the story led to my first mistake; I called the number listed in the house organ and asked to speak to the scientist in charge," said Loory. The scientist referred him to the institute's information officer "for all the information."

After explaining that he seldom found the information offices with all the information, Loory thought he had arranged an interview through the information office. The information officer offered Loory a fact sheet nine months old. The information officer also said he did not think he could disturb scientists in their laboratories. Loory took the fact sheet for background and persisted in his request for interviews. The information officer said he could fill in the information. "I suggested that a call to the office of the NIH Director James Shannon might ease the way," Loory reported. From this call, Loory got an hour-and-a-half interview with an associate director of NIAID.

> The session was filled with a reasonable amount of general information . . . but not enough for a major feature such as I planned. The interview finished, I asked for the tour of the laboratory. Impossible they [sic] said in unison. "You can't disturb the scientists in their laboratories." Once again I appealed the ruling to NIH headquarters, but this time even that maneuver did not work. . . .

> The scientists, all working in unclassified government laboratories and paid with government funds, stood determined to keep their doors closed and all the pleading of public relations experts and administrators could not coax them open.

With the NIH information officer's knowledge, Loory took his problem to the assistant to the surgeon general for information. "He did not even bother to return my call." Loory next appealed to the assistant to the secretary of Health, Education and Welfare for public affairs. A laboratory tour was approved. As Loory described the experience:

I arrived . . . and found that two administrators—one a scientist and the other an "executive secretary"—would take me on the tour. I also found they had allotted a whole half hour to the distasteful business which meant that when I stopped to talk to people in the lab I was literally pulled away by the shoulder. The scientists running the laboratory were conveniently absent and the technicians notably reticent about discussing their work.

Toward the end of my travail, the NIAID information officer did supply me with a list of all the grantees around the country working in the vaccine development program and eventually, using this list, the telephone and a visit to Children's Hospital in Washington, I gathered enough information to write a story.

I think newsmen and the general public—the master the newsmen serve in *cooperation* with government information officers—deserve better treatment from the men who hold the keys to the truth in government agencies.

Loory deserves a medal for his tenacity and the variety of approaches he used to extract information.

It is worth noting that encounters between the press and government technical agencies seemed to increase in the spring of 1961. This followed the U.S.-supported invasion of Cuba by anti-Castro rebels and a speech by President John F. Kennedy. The President urged the American Newspaper Publishers Association on April 27, 1961, to impose a self-censorship on news that might aid Communist countries (187:1).

In May, Robert S. McNamara promised the Senate Armed Services Committee, according to censored testimony from closed hearings, that he would reduce disclosure of military information "of benefit to our potential enemies" (196:1).

In the Senate transcript, McNamara had stated that the Nike-Zeus rocket weapon against ballistic missiles and the Midas "spy-in-the-sky" satellite were of doubtful effectiveness.

By June, the United Press International reported an "information blackout" on the nuclear-powered cruiser *Long Beach* nearing completion.

The only break in what seemed to be a growing information barrier came from Congressman John E. Moss. Moss was offended by a statement by the Civil Service Commission directive to all government employees which read: "Employees may not disclose official information without either appropriate general or specific authority under agency regulations" (82:15).

Declared Moss in a letter to Frederick G. Dutton, special assistant to President Kennedy: "Federal employees have a duty to make available Government information unless there is a compelling reason for withholding the information."

Perhaps these incidents were only coincidental aftermaths of the President's speech to newspaper editors. After the speech, the President met with several leading editors, publishers and press association executives. They agreed on a joint statement, *The New York Times* reported. "The President assured the group that the Administration intends to continue its policy of free access to the news and that no form of restriction is contemplated or suggested" (196:14).

In private conversations, however, at least a dozen science writers have said they felt a change in attitude during the summer of 1961. They were unsure whether information was being restricted by high authority or, perhaps, that lesser officials had been emboldened to experiment with their own news controls.

Years later *The New York Times* executives admitted their reporters had enough information to print an accurate picture of U.S. movements leading to the Cuban Bay of Pigs invasion. Instead the editors overrode their reporters' objections and killed the story at the request of ranking government officials. The decision, the editors recalled with bitterness, was wrong (251).

And by 1970 even nuclear secrecy seemed too much of a social burden to Dr. Edward Teller, one of the men who helped install and support one of the most elaborate security systems outside Russia and China. It was Dr. Teller who figured in the celebrated Oppenhimer Case of security review, who helped develop the H-Bomb and who was an advisor on weaponry for the antiballistic missile system. He wrote:

A quarter-century of experience should have taught us that a democracy cannot function effectively under a cloak of secrecy; that secrecy impedes the flow and exchange of knowledge and dampens the productivity of scientific research [253].

Secrecy, he maintained, cost the U.S. leadership in nuclear weapons while its removal for nuclear power reactors allowed full scientific participation and produced unmatched results. Secrecy alienates the best scientists at the best universities from working on national defense problems. Secrecy as official policy, he maintained, confuses discussions of military preparedness and robs the public of understanding while hampering potential antagonists very little. And secrecy, misused, has brought about the tag of "credibility gap" (a fancy word for lying) which has been applied to federal pronouncements at many levels for a decade.

International Ties

International commitments also complicate the flow of information about scientific and technical projects. An increasing number of purely scientific undertakings are modeled on the International Geophysical Year agreements in force in 1957. NASA operates tracking stations, training programs and space exploration projects with other nations. Diplomacy requires coordination with the allied country before details are discussed with newsmen. Practicality demands some coordination of announcements to ensure success. Difficulty with stories that involve other countries may be expected. This does not necessarily mean that the agency is withholding information for other reasons. The science writer should satisfy himself, however, that this restriction is legitimate. Diplomacy need not be an overriding consideration to the exclusion of all other reasons for obtaining a story.

American scientific and technical accomplishments are also the material for building our image abroad. The U.S. Information Agency, known overseas as the U.S. Information Service, plays particular court to foreign science writers. Information officers overseas have a five-point approach to establishing and maintaining rapport between the USIS and these foreign science writers. The program involves:

1. Providing background material and photographs of American scientific achievements.
2. Helping to plan reporting trips to the United States.
3. Arranging special film showings on science subjects.
4. Distributing USIA-NASA Science Writers Service.
5. Inviting writers to meet American scientists.

This overseas program seldom touches the domestic science writer except to provide the opportunity to meet some interesting writers at American science conventions and other events. These writers are either foreign nationals brought to America or USIA writers who specialize in science coverage. American writers overseas have reported that free USIA stories are direct competition for story sales to foreign publications.

About the only point of conflict for the American science writer in the USIS activities involves competition for interviews. It is a personal observation, shared by other writers, that visiting science writers receive priority in interviewing U.S. scientists. This is understandable. The visitors have only limited time. They are escorted by a Department of State official, on many occasions, to government centers around the country.

A powerful persuader for immediate cooperation with USIS is the need for other agencies, NASA in particular, to secure favors in return from the State Department. A writer should be aware of this situation and prepare himself to be inconvenienced by it occasionally. On occasion one can arrange a little extra cooperation, feeding questions to the foreign science writer who stands a better chance of getting an answer on certain subjects.

Military, Politics and Science

Any science writer who thinks the science field will cause him to miss political assignments has a surprise coming. Political questions merely appear in somewhat different guise for the science writer than for the legislative reporter. New and experimental weapons in the space-atomic age represent advances in applied science, clothed in political relationships.

New weapons naturally involve security regulations. While most reporters are not automatically bound by security, as defined by the Department of Defense, many news sources are. Science writers in military reserve units may find themselves restricted more than other writers when challenging security regulations to obtain a story.

No special laws govern publication of classified information. However, the writer is subject to prosecution, in a court trial, for possessing classified material or for deliberately endangering the national security. However, it must be proved that the writer knowingly jeopardized the national security. The science writer's chief protection is that he seldom has any use for detailed information about how to build or use most lethal devices. These details are indescribably boring for a mass audience.

Self-censorship is common among writers who accidentally receive information that might endanger national security. This author once withheld the story that a large number of Strategic Air Command bombers had been damaged severely by a freak hailstorm. Robert Hotz and his *Aviation Week* writers knew about a new Mach 3.5 military aircraft for more than two years before it was announced by President Lyndon B. Johnson in 1964. The only recognition given by *Aviation Week* before the official announcement was to mention the designer by name in citing him "for his continued ingenuity" (102:11).

A reporter has little difficulty in deciding not to write a story once he's convinced national security is involved. More difficult, however, is deciding whether the need for classification is real. The military establishment, like any other bureaucracy, may classify facts because of policy matters, possible embarrassment or political decisions.

President Johnson may be the only president who seemingly declassified the same airplane twice, once as an interceptor and again as a reconnaissance aircraft. The occurrences, first in March and then in July of the 1964 campaign year, moved Hotz to comment:

The "SR-71" was, of course, the A-11 with still another designation pasted on its titanium skin. But many congressmen were fooled, and unthinking daily newspapermen and wire service reporters failed to catch the deception and spread the news across the nation of the "new" billion-dollar aircraft program . . .

The inception of this program also was conveniently shifted from 1959 in the Eisenhower Administration to 1963 in the Kennedy Administration. Anyone familiar with aircraft development cycles knows that if this program were really started in 1963, it would be impossible to deliver operational aircraft to Strategic Air Command in 1965 as President Johnson stated.

We suspect that the next chapter in the checkered career of the A-11 will be the "revelation" at the most opportune political moment that it can be a bomber, too . . . [104:11].

The magazine and others also raised serious questions as to how a government was able to finance secretly an aircraft development program without some public accounting of tens of millions of dollars spent on the project (248:16).

Outright lying probably is rare among officials. The science writer is in good position to examine public statements cloaked in highly technical language. Hotz, whose staff works closely with the military, has some strong words on this point. His stand seems most courageous because his magazine depends in a large part upon military men as news sources.

Here's how Hotz feels:

Lack of credibility of key government officials is always a serious matter in a democratic society. . . . This may prove to be an extremely high price for President Johnson to pay for whatever succes Mr. McNamara and his official mouthpiece, Arthur Sylvester, have achieved in their avowed intent to control Pentagon news to suit their own purposes. This policy backfired badly in the Cuban crisis. . . . Both . . . came to their Pentagon duties with an unusual belief in the use of the official lie as a national policy instrument. Mr. McNamara first made this clear in 1961 testimony before Congress on Nike-Zeus (an anti-missile system) when he said: "Why should we tell Russia that Zeus developments may not be satisfactory? What we ought to be saying is that we have the most perfect anti-ICBM system that the human mind will ever devise."

Pentagon reporters really don't believe a story until it has been officially denied. Even his (Sylvester) subordinates are apologetic for the more blatant episodes.

Mr. Sylvester's internal Pentagon directive to all military public information officers ordering the F-111 to be portrayed publicly as a success . . . would read more appropriately in the Cyrillic alphabet than in English. The idea of proclaiming that an aircraft will meet all of the military service requirements before the first prototype has rolled out or made its initial flight is so ludicrous it belongs in a George Orwell book.

Clearly it is time . . . for a realistic examination of an official information policy that is widening the gap between a government and its people at a critical time in the fate of this nation [103:21].

One more vignette serves to illustrate this particular kind of pitfall that awaits the science writer in the land of the military. Earlier it was noted that McNamara had told the U.S. Senate he had serious doubts about the Nike-Zeus rocket system. On Thursday, September 17, 1964, President Johnson announced in Sacramento, California, that the United States had two weapons capable of intercepting any enemy satellite (260:1).

Friday, at a special press conference, McNamara disclosed that the Army's system of satellite interception was based on the Nike-Zeus. And, he said, the once-maligned Nike-Zeus had been operational or combat-ready for more than a year, since August 1, 1963 (223:4).

President Johnson's opponent, Senator Barry Goldwater, had been accusing the administration of failure to develop new weapons. After Johnson's disclosure, Goldwater charged, on Saturday, that the President had used "highly classified defense information in purely political manner" (86:12). A decade later, military engineers were still developing a workable missile interceptor. Selective release of classified information is common.

Science writers should not brood too long, lest they become cynical—an offense often attributed to newspaper writers in general. However, in the happy age of positive thinking, the science writer should maintain a broad streak of political skepticism.

New secrecy in the conduct of American affairs was not unexpected. The blackout had started long before President Kennedy's speech to the newspaper publishers. On February 10, 1961, officials stopped releasing tracking data on Russian satellites over the United States. The authority to do so stemmed from an order dated November, 1960, said Pentagon spokesmen (269:12). ("Spokesmen" almost always means the Pentagon public affairs personnel—formerly called information officers.)

This was followed by an April, 1961, directive from Sylvester forbidding discussion of any missile launchings unless they were witnessed by the public. In addition, Sylvester classified the guidance memorandum itself as "for official use only" (268:21), denying newsmen an opportunity to see the order.

Jules Witcover of the Newhouse News Service in Washington has chronicled the effects of mutual distrust between information officers and newsmen. In the Pentagon, reporters learn they will get an answer to the questions they ask, but the answer may not be amplified to cover any question that is not asked specifically.

News sources must be built within—and even against—the biggest, most complex and often most hostile system in Washington. The effect has been to produce a press corps with a chip on its collective shoulders and the acid, penetrating ability to cross-examine with questions a defense attorney would envy.

In the city of the easy handout . . . their independence and their integrity compare favorably with that of reporters on other Washington beats. They are neither more ethical nor less responsible—just a good deal more ornery. They play ball in a league where it pays to examine the ball after each pitch, and they've acquired the habit [280:15].

On the positive side, federal officers will extend amazing amounts of assistance under certain conditions—every public relations man likes a favorable story.

When it comes to classified information, investigators may follow the advice of Joseph and Stewart Alsop, given in *The Reporter's Trade* (7:58-77): A reporter should not only refrain from examining any classified document, but in the unlikely case that one is shown to him, he should not reproduce language from that document.

No matter how arcane the subject, enough has always been printed about it in non-classified publications to give you a general idea of the right questions [7:66].

On the other hand, classification in the 1970 decade appeared to be so all-pervasive, so arbitrarily applied and so easily lifted when it served political purposes that many journalists have grown less concerned with the security stamp as a meaningful symbol. Columnist Jack Anderson and Neil Sheehan of the *New York Times* won journalism's highest prizes for deliberately printing material from classified files about the Vietnam conflict, and the Nixon Administration revised classification authority to reduce the amount of material put under security stamp.

Howard Simons, now managing editor of *The Washington Post* and winner of the 1964 Westinghouse award for science writing, covered the physical sciences and the "public policy" stories in the capital.

He makes these points about science news coverage (202:17):

1. You must write for young readers who care about science and their parents who want to understand the politics of scientific developments. Coverage of science as politics is "far sexier and more personally rewarding."

2. You can read a story back to a scientist for corrections of fact; "I'd rather have great accuracy than great prose."

3. A "scoop" is not easily defined in science news. He gets some stories first because only he has the time to pay particular attention to a project or agency.
4. The science writer can piece "little dribs and drabs of information" into a coherent story about a classified subject without violating national security.
5. Control of science in public policy should remain in the hands of politicians. "The amateur is far better than the expert as far as I am concerned."
6. The writer can become too expert; he must retain some of the ignorance of the inquiring reporter.

The Scientific Adviser

Another center of great power, operating in semi-secrecy, was pinpointed (1:1-17) by Dr. Philip H. Abelson, director of the geophysical laboratory of the Carnegie Institution. The President's scientific adviser serves as a personal counsel to the President, heads the President's Science Advisory Committee, serves as director of the office of Science and Technology and also acts as chairman of the Federal Council on Science and Technology.

Because part of his work is to coordinate research, the science adviser (Dr. Jerome B. Wiesner at that time) is director of the Bureau of the Budget where scientific matters are concerned.

Even the most powerful agency head must make his peace with the science adviser lest his budget suffer. I know of no evidence that this budgetary power has been misused, but its very existence cannot but color relations between the adviser and the various agencies of the government [1:8].

Times change. Although the science adviser in 1970 retained the three jobs, criticism indicated that power in the office was easily withdrawn by the President. John Lannan of *The Washington Star* and other science writers were admitted to a briefing by Dr. Lee A. DuBridge. Most of the time was devoted to the science adviser's defense of U.S. science policy against criticism, by scientists, that the policy was both weak and ineffective. And, the critics suggested, the same might be said for the adviser and his staff (134).

Dr. Abelson's own recommendation was to divide this power among several persons to reduce the concentration of power. He also asked that more of the activities of the Office of Science and Technology be brought into the public domain for examination.

This conflict between the demands for freedom of information and the restrictions of a bureaucracy goes on at all levels. Examples may be found in other U.S. agencies and in state, county and city agencies.

The Space Agency

The information activities of NASA deserve special attention. Its rapid growth made it one of the major dispensers of tax funds.

The large NASA budgets permit the agency to extend its influence into almost every sphere of physical and biological science. The agency's needs are large in addition to any bureaucratic "empire building" that may take place concurrently with research.

For these reasons, hardly any science writer can escape dealing with NASA. Its information practices, already under fire by science writers, hold a special interest.

The act establishing the agency specifically directs that its administrators shall "provide for the widest practicable and appropriate dissemination of information concerning its activities and the results thereof" (165:5).

The question arises: Should public funds be used to shape public opinion at home? A line between desirable public information and undesirable influence is difficult to draw. Francis E. Rourke reviews the question thoroughly in his *Secrecy and Publicity, Dilemmas of Democracy* (204:1-198).

Vernon Van Dyke in a study of the rationale of the space program found the space agency tends to overemphasize the secrecy provisions of its enabling legislation at the expense of its informational mandate (271:71). The NASA information policies are far from being as rigidly patterned as are those of the century-old National Academy of Sciences-National Research Council. NASA policies which hamper working newsmen can be hammered into a more acceptable form by vigilant, aggressive and vocal writers. Van Dyke observed (271:254) that NASA's voluminous public information activity tends to be objective and factual rather than thematic.

Contract Restrictions

Every legal contract signed by NASA and many other agencies contains the seed of censorship. This is a clause reading:

> The Contractor agrees that it shall not release any public statements or news releases regarding this contract without prior clearance with the Contracting Officer. The Contractor further agrees to insert the provisions of this clause in any subcontract requiring the prior written approval of the Contracting Officer [61].

This means that any contractor and his employees must submit speeches, press releases, pictures and pamphlets or brochures to the Public Affairs Office at the NASA center supervising the contract. Approval must be given in writing by the Public Affairs Officer, the purchasing officer assigned to the contract and the engineer or technical person who authorized the contract. NASA officials cite two reasons for this requirement. One is to prevent "premature release" of information; the other is to insure accuracy.

The contract provision handicaps the flow of information two ways: (a) reporters cannot check rumors or reports directly with the contractor, and (b) it restricts development of new facts by limiting discussions with the people doing the work to facts approved by NASA for public consumption.

It would seem that there might be a conflict between a "fact" as seen by an engineer working on a project and a "fact" as seen through the eyes of a space-age federal administrator.

The practice is not limited to NASA's agreements with commercial contractors. It may be argued that commercial contracts involve devices with military value. But the technique is applied to universities doing scientific research and to cooperative projects with other branches of the government.

Since agency imitates agency, other civilian departments coming new into research and development have kept similar restrictions when they have gone unchallenged. One of the newer tactics has been to label reports "internal documents." In theory an internal document concerns the formative stages of policy; in practice, the difference between an external and internal document often lies only in the official decision to make it public.

The author once attempted to gain details about a telescope proposed by NASA for an university observatory. University officials could not discuss the project without NASA approval. The information officer, theoretically installed to help prevent misunderstandings, offered no clarification beyond a potential diameter of "80-150 inches." Unless NASA scientists were being sloppy, this was much too great a range of indecision to exist only one step away from final approval. Calling a congressman on the NASA appropriations committee produced the answer very rapidly from the political liaison man at the space agency.

(Moral: When you're stuck with a doubtful "official" answer, call the most powerful U.S. senator or representative you know.)

A similar restriction on other government agencies came to light in an unusual way. After thorough research on the ways astronauts are selected, this author interviewed doctors at the Air Force School of Aviation Medicine where the men received their physical examinations. Following publication of the stories, one of the doctors wrote asking for a letter explaining that the pictures and background information used with the stories did not come from the Air Force but from NASA's own information office. The doctor said the Air Force had been accused by NASA officials of violating an agreement that only NASA would release astronaut photographs (142). The material had, in fact, come from NASA information files.

(Moral: Don't limit yourself to only one official source of information. A "fact" that is restricted in one place frequently is unclassified information at another.*)*

The extent of the review of information that NASA requires is illustrated by a two-page memorandum on procedures given Manned Spacecraft Center contractors:

> In conformance with the National Aeronautics and Space Act [sic] of 1958, the National Aeronautics and Space Administration will provide the widest appropriate dissemination of information on scientific, unclassified activities.
>
> a. All information material proposed for release by contractors, suppliers, and vendors must be submitted to NASA for review and approval prior to release. This material includes: news releases, still photographs, artwork, advertising, motion pictures, displays and exhibits, TV clips, speeches, public appearance requests, news conference plans, requests for commercial use of still and motion pictures, technical articles, and papers. . . .
>
> d. Material pertaining to the Gemini launch and target vehicles . . . must be reviewed by both MSC and the Air Force Space Systems division.
>
> f. All material should be received by MSC at least 15 days prior to desired [sic] release time. . . .
>
> g. Contractors, suppliers, and vendors . . . may respond to query, utilizing material which is currently accurate and previously cleared for release [148:1].

The Honest Quote

A good, honest quote from a news source is increasingly hard to obtain. Agencies tend to allow personnel to speak only through the anonymous words of press agents.

In October, 1963, the Russians intimated that they might not be pursuing a lunar landing project. The following wire went out from Julian Scheer of NASA headquarters to all information officers.

UNCLAS X ATTN TO ALL PIO'S URGENT CALL HOMES UR DUTY OFFICERS X THIS STATEMENT BY NASA ON RUSSIAN STATE-MENT. NO FURTHER COMMENT: ...... MAKE IT UNATTRIBUTED BUT TO NASA. NOTE HOLD UNTIL CONFIRMED BY AP. WILL NOTIFY YOU [206].

No reporter could talk to officials of NASA anywhere in the world and receive anything but one stiff, formal statement.

Similarly, it's worth noticing how stiltedly astronaut Donald K. Slayton spoke through a news release from Ames Research Center in California:

Ultimate fidelity in simulating various phases of a manned space mission has been an engineering goal of the [Gemini] program since its inception. We are using the centrifuge at Ames because it is the only one in the country capable of superimposing the stresses we are interested in [8:1].

This NASA announcement was interesting for another reason. Slayton and other astronauts swung between California and Pennsylvania during this mid-July period of 1963. They were whirled violently aboard the human centrifuges at Ames and at the Johnsville, Pennsylvania, Navy center. Houston's NASA officials described the purpose as a "routine training activity."

The Houston information officer who accompanied them to Johnsville said the visit was to conduct the first tests of certain equipment under high gravity forces. "She [the information officer] declined to identify specific items of equipment being tested," said an Associated Press report.

The press release from Ames Research Center gave a slightly different, and more honest, account.

In accordance with NASA's philosophy of investigating every conceivable aspect of space flight, the tests at Ames are designed to determine the astronauts' *ability to read vital instruments under conditions which may occur during the mission* [italics mine]. The astronauts' reaction under stress was exercised during the tests [8:1].

A confidential call to an MSC engineer in Houston, definitely not a public affairs officer, gave an even more direct answer. The men were being rattled on these centrifuges in a simulated so-called "pogo-stick effect" produced by the launching rocket. The tests were to determine if the pilots could control the spaceship if this vibration could not be removed.

Control of the People

Access to people also controls lively quotes and basic information. Government officials impose several types of controls and they shift constantly. Identification badges that differ markedly from agency or contractor employees' badges give a visual signal that says "outsider" when issued to a writer. Scientists may be forbidden to talk directly to a newsman who calls unless the call has been approved in advance by an information officer. Both the Department of Defense and the National Institutes of Health have required staff scientists to report all conversations with journalists or fellow scientists acting in the capacity of mass media writers. When a scientist, engineer or administrator is suspected of being too frank, the information officer may substitute a more manage-able news source for the one requested.

In some times of crisis, when development projects are politi-cally "hot," men actually working on the project may be forbid-den to give interviews. Then all comments come from political appointees. Queries in such cases are answered by men who know more about policy than about the real scientific or engineering problems. Another form of restriction is to have a "monitor" or third party sit through the interview.

At early space flights, newsmen coming to the Manned Space-craft Center were handed ground rules that included this: "Inter-views with Manned Spacecraft Center personnel in Houston will not be authorized during the mission . . ." Time, experience and confidence quickly eroded this directive.

Time also ended the block contracts by which all astronauts agreed to sell their personal stories to Field Enterprises and Life. However, individual astronauts and other government officials may be bound on occasion by contracts with their own publishers or other outlets. Adm. Hyman Rickover, for example, has fought a long battle to retain publication rights to all his speeches and statements. Indeed, it has become rather common for publishers and networks to pay handsomely for rights of "exclusive" access to people participating in newsworthy events.

Quite often the effect of these restrictions is minimal. They set off a ritualistic *gavotte* in which the writer calls the news source and arranges the interview. Or his contact may arrange an interview with a more qualified person. Then the reporter calls the information officer and requests an interview at a particular time with a specific person. Another tactic for similarly "locking-in" an interview is to ask a ranking official for his recommendation on someone who can give additional information.

Pity the PR Man

Relations between the newsmen and the government public relations men are often very cordial. And in many instances the information officer is more to be pitied than condemned. He cannot compel a person to be interviewed, and some government scientists and engineers genuinely feel they are wasting their time with reporters or that the resulting story will always reflect badly on them or their agency.

Government public relations officers, particularly NASA employees, may be forbidden to release information (a) by order of a high ranking executive who is not an information man or (b) because of the classification stamped on the document. The publicity man disregards these elements at the risk of his job. The space agency, unlike the Air Force, has no published set of regulations specifying what may and may not be given newsmen.

These restrictions are understood by generally sympathetic newsmen. In cases where neither controversy nor classification is involved, public relations men have made great efforts to help a reporter. Any action that clears away even part of this jungle of information barriers must be applauded—loudly.

Commando Tactics

Science writers, with their technical knowledge, can evade many restrictive practices. An arsenal of weapons exists for the writer willing to use them. It is no misnomer to refer to the following practices as "commando tactics." They produce accurate, newsworthy stories without the approval or even cooperation of government administrative and information officers. In fact, these tactics will produce stories over the active opposition of an imperfect bureaucracy.

Find and learn to use the "bid board" of the agency or center involved. This is where all federal and most state contracting officers must post notices announcing that they need certain equipment or services and will accept bids on a specified date. Questionable practices in awarding public contracts have brought business pressure to make all but the most highly classified contracts a matter of public notice and record. Anyone may inspect these announcements without asking any government official. These "requests for proposal" (RFP) and "request for quotation" (RFQ) notices also describe the purposes of the material and other background facts. Federal contracting officers risk much more if they withhold information on a public contract than does an information officer.

Develop tipsters. After knowledge of the procedures for spending public funds, the writer's most valuable asset is people who will tell him of events, facts or plans. Tipsters do not have to be "important" people. They do not necessarily deliberately "give" information, although few reliable people drop scraps of fact accidentally. Accidents do happen, however, and one must stay alert for the unexpected "tip." An important news story revealing serious design problems in the world's largest and most expensive vacuum chamber resulted from a chance encounter with an accidental tipster (42:1). *Check all tips thoroughly.*

Read the scientific or technical journals. Beginning in 1946, Joseph and Stewart Alsop spent months studying all the published data on atomic physics, reactors and weapons. From their reading they found that the feasibility of a hydrogen bomb had been discussed for more than four years in the open literature. From this background they were able to break the story of the H-bomb's possession by both Russia and the United States (7:62).

As mentioned, scientists and research engineers tend to give their stories first to their professional publications. When a local researcher has published his technical paper, he is usually ready to talk about it to the popular press. If a reporter has a name and a background of understanding, hardly anyone can stop him from getting an interview. Often men in the headquarters of an agency will publish a report dealing with work on the local level; this itself opens the subject locally. The boss has removed the classification at the highest level.

Study the trade publications. Industrial magazines charge heavily for their advertising, and writers for the trade press must deliver usable information that is newsworthy and accurate. Like tips, these stories should be rechecked.

Know your congressmen, senators and their staffs. Most agencies and many local centers have political liason men. Working through these, elected officials often secure information forbidden to public relations men for general release. It is also political courtesy for agencies to allow elected officials to announce new projects.

Inspect purchase orders. Like contracts, purchase orders are public record; these usually list just a general description of the items bought, the number of the purchase and who authorized it, and which company received the money. Much of this is dull reading, but unusual purchases, the large amounts of money and even the unusual small items can be turned into stories ranging from short "brights" to a major story. For instance, a transfer of funds under NASA contract NAS 9-1396 led to discovery that the Manned Spacecraft Center was having difficulty building a space suit that would be adequate for use by Project Gemini astronauts (200).

Develop contacts in other branches of an agency. Engineering and information officers at one location may talk freely about certain work while those at another consider the topic classified.

Similarly, one branch of government may discuss related work in another division.

Attend meetings. Growing numbers of scientific and technical personnel have produced a similar growth in the number of professional societies. Engineers and others involved in government programs appear as speakers. A reporter can arrange for notices of speakers and invitations through local chapter officers. He risks sitting through a technical and even dull speech, although often the speech itself is newsworthy. The occasion offers the reporter the opportunity to meet the speaker without a monitor from the information office.

Monitor scientific conventions. By keeping track of scientific society annual meetings, the reporter also knows where and when researchers are speaking. Knowing the name of the speaker, his topic and his speaking date opens the door to request a copy of the speech from the speaker or the organization he is to address. An interview before or after the speech may also be requested.

Collect center newspapers, house organs, official notices and press releases. Internal information officers publish much material for government employees. By reading base newspapers, center house organs and daily bulletins, the reporter uses these internal information people as legmen to gather tips and story information. Several years ago this author was denied an official report about the cause of a fatal airplane accident. Shortly afterward, while strolling past a bulletin board, he noticed a large colored flight-safety poster that detailed the cause of the accident. Each internal publication, notice or press release contains some information that will fit into a larger picture.

Frequent public areas of the installation. Cafeterias, base exchanges, portions of the flight operations towers and libraries are semipublic places for the convenience of visitors to military and civilian installations. These visitors often have no more official access to classified information or restricted areas than the reporter. This author deliberately chooses to have coffee, eat or perform some literature research at these unrestricted places. There are two reasons: (a) people get used to seeing him and accept his presence, and (b) these locations offer a good vantage point to observe distinguished visitors who may not have been announced.

Exercise your imagination. A reporter should try to see more than one possibility hidden in the general information about capabilities of various space or atomic devices. For example, Maxime Faget, spacecraft designer, depicted a great many peaceful uses for the Project Apollo spaceships in an article written for *The Houston Chronicle's Texas* rotogravure section (73:58-59). It was no great trick to use this and other background information on Project Apollo to produce, after some extensive checking, an article pointing out the potential military applications for Apollo (48:2).

Secure annual reports of the bureaus and agencies within your scope. These provide story ideas as well as a starting point for story research. The annual report of the Atomic Energy Commission covers atomic weapons, reactor design, nuclear submarines and uranium production. A letter to the agency headquarters will put one on the mailing list. Almost all of these reports list research grants and the scientists supported by the agency.

Acquaint yourself with private scientific information sources. The *Space Log* from Space Technology Laboratories, Redondo Beach, California, rounds up all Russian and American satellite launches. In several cities scientists have formed "scientists information committees." Their primary concern is with the effects of nuclear energy, including fallout and civil defense. Members will also discuss other general aspects of scientific and applied research. Their semipolitical efforts are coordinated by the Scientists Committee on Radiation Information working through the New York Academy of Sciences (152:1-25).

Study Congressional testimony. One of the NASA's most closely guarded "non-secrets" was its tentative schedule for landing astronauts on the moon. By reading 3,540 pages of testimony before the U.S. House of Representatives Committee on Science and Astronautics (161:1-3540), the rough timetable could be deduced. The timetable revealed that the earliest possible time for a lunar landing was in the fall of 1968 (43:5).

These printed texts of testimony appear months after witnesses go before the committees. This time lapse does not mean that the information is outdated. Erratic news coverage of the testimony allows only the sketchiest accounts beyond the Washington area. Information should be checked with the agency involved, however, to see if the programs have been changed. Events since the testimony may have produced major alterations; these changes or the effects of these events are news stories in themselves.

For the beginning writer, the Congressional testimony is a good place to learn about his new field. Since Congressmen seldom have technical backgrounds, scientists couch their explanations in most understandable terms. The Congressmen, in turn, ask many questions about the programs to better understand the agency's needs.

Committee staffs also turn out a variety of other publications the writer may use. *The Practical Values of Space Exploration* (189) remains useful years after printing.

Cracking Secrecy: A Case Study

Most of these tactics were used in 1970 to assemble a story the military refused to discuss. It did not concern science but a new and dramatic application of some very advanced technology. This story grew, in fact, out of the author's irritation over a rather high-handed refusal by the Army to elaborate upon a subject it had used twice in publicity ploys. Eventually it became part of the Senate debate on military spending.

On October 14, 1969, Gen. William C. Westmoreland, Army chief of staff, spoke to the Association of the U.S. Army about "a quiet revolution in ground warfare—tactics, techniques and technology. This revolution is not fully understood. . . ." Later he announced formation of task forces, at the Pentagon and at Fort Hood, Texas, to devise and test the whole range of military operations based upon devices known as "remote sensors." One remote sensor is the light-amplifying television tube, a device the author had first heard about from astronomers. They used it to increase the power of their telescopes by magnifying the light from stars too far away and too faint for viewing. Other vague stories had floated around about the use of microphones, tiny seismographs, glowing chemicals, magnetometers, "people sniffers" and other gear in Vietnam.

At this point the author was interested only in a story about the Army's test plans. But the Army "does not choose to discuss the matter at this time," reported the information officer who tried to arrange an interview with the Army's project officer. The military considered the matter closed. A written request to General Westmoreland brought a more polite reply, but no action. All signs said: "Run-around."

Meanwhile the author was doing other stories. While visiting an Army lab outside Washington, he was given a short report about researchers testing new ways to make small combat groups as effective as battalions and divisions. Sure enough, remote sensors and all the other electronic gear played an important role in giving the small group the firepower, accuracy and control of a much larger force of men. There was an article, he was told, back in August, 1969, in *Army* magazine; the author was a general who directed early research in surveillance, target acquisition and night operations equipment; his group helped adapt delicate scientific instrumentation for rugged field usage by untrained combat troops. (One question answered.)

The author reread General Westmoreland's speech and the *Army* article. A house organ printed at another base provided some answers about how many men the Ft. Hood tests involved, when they would start and how the project was organized. (There were more answers.)

The literature turned up reference to a "Defense Communications Planning Group" led by a lieutenant general. A request for an interview brought only the word that the chief of defense information, an Army colonel, had ordered no interview and no discussion of the DCPG. (An information officer pointed out that DCPG was listed in the Pentagon telephone directory and a shuttle bus carrying the DCPG emblem made hourly runs between the Pentagon and the group's offices at the Naval Observatory in Washington.)

Next came a check of a technical news service published by McGraw-Hill for contractors. Under "Electronic Battlefield" appeared a detailed listing of the overall aims of the effort, the amount of money spent in public contracts and who was building what kinds of sensors. Now this author had a frame of references—and the picture was much bigger than the Army's one project. What was emerging was this: How a small attempt to find guerrillas at night grew into an R&D effort that had consumed nearly $3 billion in a few years, involved the Army, Navy, Air Force and the Advanced Research Projects Agency and opened the way to a completely new style of warfare for all services. (Answers—but they were unconfirmed; nothing had come from the requests for interviews.)

Then the author decided to let congressmen and senators do his interviewing. He began reading the hearings of the armed services and appropriations committees in the House and Senate. (Only laziness kept him from this earlier; the thousands of pages of testimony filled more than a dozen volumes.) Despite security classifications, a lot of material, including usable quotes, was drawn out by the legislators. However, there were great blanks in the testimony where statements had been omitted for security reasons. Also, it developed, that nowhere—unless in censored statements—had witnesses from the Department of Defense rolled all their efforts into one comprehensive picture for Congress. (Now the story assumed a much larger importance: Congress authorizing a billion dollar expense without anyone outside a small group of committee members having a full view of the effort.)

Further reading showed that the military censors had left uncensored in several places the facts, figures, descriptions, etc., that had been stricken from the record in other places. By comparing testimony from all sources (House, Senate, two Armed Services Committees and two Appropriations Committees), most of the blank spots could be filled. Each fact was simply put on a sheet of paper and the notes were separated into related topics: infrared imaging, low-light television, airborne sensors, helicopters, malfunctions, computer displays, etc. Quotes by the men-who-wouldn't-talk could be related to these subjects. This page-by-page assembly turned up official estimates on cost, failure and success.

In original testimony these were often censored so that only cross-volume comparisons could relate them. While hardly as satisfactory as a series of personal interviews, the research at this time contained factual data and authoritative quotes needed for a story. The story could have been written now. However, the material gave the author a grasp of the subject and confidence to approach the individual services to ask for visits to the labs and testing grounds. One request paid off with a background briefing on many technical problems and applications. Then another thought coalesced: Full integration of sensors, airplanes, ground troops, displays, etc., almost certainly predicted the use of computer systems to connect all this together. A computer project manager revealed that he was indeed altering the direction and physical location of two computer R&D projects to fit into the "automated battlefield" concept. Contacting the contractors involved produced a few more bits of information and pictures; these had been cleared for publication, usually in house organs.

The story appeared in two McGraw-Hill magazines: *Business Week* on January 31, 1970, and *Product Engineering,* February 16, 1970.

How little Congress knew of the scope and size and spread of the electronic surveillance effort was shown on July 7, 1970, more than five months after publication. Sen. William Proxmire entered a critical speech in the Congressional Record; Sen. Barry Goldwater said the program was "so highly classified that even the Armed Services Committee has not been able to hold hearings on it." Sen. Stuart Symington claimed that he had been told by military men the subject was too sensitive for discussion even in executive session.

Stung by implications that he had revealed classified information, Senator Proxmire entered the texts of the *Business Week* and *Product Engineering* articles, and other public source material, into the *Congressional Record* of July 13, 1970 (pp. S-11102 through S-11116). To answer Senator Proxmire and show some "classified" material for the record, Senator Goldwater had the Air Force working for two days on pulling together, for the first time, most of the costs of the scattered projects (*Congressional Record,* July 15, 1970). Even then he did not get all of it from the Air Force files; omitted were costs for night vision devices and for explosives connected with the electronic sensors.

Summary

A reporter can become practically independent of news or information controls through these techniques. For an investigative or analytical story, the sources cited here provide indispensable documentation. How vigorously one utilizes these techniques will depend on how badly one needs them.

The relationship between an information officer and a writer often works. Then stories come easily, and the writer can consider himself very lucky. When the situation is less ideal, the writer need not feel completely dependent upon the information man.

When writers feel they are being excessively curbed, they may appeal to Congress. The place to file such a protest is with a subcommittee of the Committee of Government Operations. This is the Government Information Plans and Policies subcommittee; it was formerly called the "Moss Committee" for its chairman, Rep. John E. Moss of California.

A protest is not always resented by government information men. They recognize, as do reporters, that restrictions by agency and center administrators end only when writers effectively demonstrate that these restrictions will not be tolerated.

John Troan has said that the hard-working, hard-reading science writer may acquire a broader understanding of scientific activity than the scientist whose movements are more limited (258:1194). The scientist moves in a path defined by his responsibilities to his personal research, the time he devotes to supervising students and research assistants, the scope of his research field and the restrictions of his travel budget.

Lawrence Lessing, science writer for *Fortune* magazine, believes that science writers and science writing should move into a broad, new and frank interpretation of science for the public (141:88-92). In accepting the James T. Grady Award Medal of the American Chemical Society, Lessing declared:

> Interpretive writing means giving the responsible, reputable science writer the same freedom of analysis, comment, and expression as that accorded a political analyst like James Reston or a foreign affairs commentator like Walter Lippmann [141:90].

Pollution of air and water, moving "backward" industries into the economic growth pattern, space and atomic defense are only a few of the public issues that require interpretation of scientific and technical potentialities and limitations.

> We need to meet these issues of science, new knowledge, and new materials squarely and with foresight. Otherwise, there are always those who are ready to throw out the baby with the bath. . . .

> Unless we do all that we can to prevent the irresponsible use of science— by governments, businesses, or people—they may succeed. And that would be a tragedy, indeed, for at its heart, we know, science is now the best hope of the world and of raising the condition of man [141:91].

This, then, is the science writer. He intends that there will be a place for him at the softening interfaces where the formerly separate fields of private and individual research tangle with public interest and public sponsorship. He stands ready to battle both the scientist-expert and the bureaucrat-expert who would restrict his role as a generalist. He also fights a rear-guard action inside the communications field to establish science's right to space, time and thoughtful public consideration. Above all he feels he can bridge the distance in understanding between the highly technical scientific society and broader culture that supports but does not comprehend the technicians' activity.

9
How to Write a Story

Science writer David Perlman of the *San Francisco Chronicle* holds one of the specialty's most coveted trophies. In 1970 Dr. John E. Cleaver of the University of California credited Perlman with setting him off on a new and successful line of research. From the information in a Perlman story, Dr. Cleaver related the effect of ultraviolet light on certain skin cancer patients to his own experiments with bacteria. Switching from bacterial to human experiments, Dr. Cleaver soon identified a missing enzyme in the cancer patients' biochemical makeup. Dr. Cleaver acknowledged his debt to popularized science writing in his formal report given to professional scientists. Perlman's story, aimed at the mass audience, conveyed enough useful scientific information to affect the course of scientific research—a superb piece of communication at all levels.

Such communication is no accident. It results from experience, judgment, organization and clarity in writing. And to a large degree the success of message transmission is determined before the writer strikes the keys of his typewriter.

Before You Write—Organize

Few stories, maybe none, "tell themselves," as writers often claim. When a reporter sits down to write his science or medical story, he has accumulated before him a literary parts kit. If he has done his work well, this kit contains more pieces than he will use. The kit includes a great many facts, some documents, specific details about the researcher and his project and history of the work. Likely his notes will contain several anecdotes about the subject; he will have quotes from his interviews with the principal investigator, maybe enough for an extended section of question-and-answer. The store of quotes may be augmented by interviews with other researchers, transcriptions from his tape recorder, testimony given in courts or at public hearings and statements made in press conferences. Where there exists an orderly, meaningful flow of events, he probably has a chronology of these events. In his mind or in his notes he has recorded also a series of scenes and impressions of the people, the places, the very atmosphere involved. Hopefully, his facts include specific details about size, height, weight, color, smell, sound, proper names, academic degrees, etc. He knows what was done, how it was done and why.

All this remains merely so much assembled material, like steel and concrete at a construction site, until he answers this question: What does it mean?

Until he has, at the least, a fairly clear answer to this question he has no story—only the pieces of one. He looks at the pieces and says: What does it mean?

This helps eliminate extraneous details. It cuts his story down to size. It enables him to assign priorities to major and minor themes, angles and directions the story may take. From this question flow all other questions that will be answered by his story.

Lewis Young, editor of *Business Week*, has contended that the facts without meaning remain merely "data." They become "information" when meaning and interpretation are applied. This is the "So What?" question framed by John Dart, science writer at

California Institute of Technology before joining *The Los Angeles Times*; "the so-what determines whether the story is written, and if so, what length and where it fits in the news report" (63).

Science writers answer this question long before the writing point, except in rare instances. Usually the source can give a concise answer. The research may advance a field of science or medicine by solving one or more mysteries, by buttressing one or another conflicting theories. A discovery may open the way to solving some problem, or it may knock down an accepted idea. Research may aid or threaten an industry, a profession or a nation.

Writers must also consider their audience. When a National Institutes of Health study suggested that diabetics using an antidiabetes drug risked early death, "What does it mean?" carried different answers for any audience that included the 800,000 Americans using the drug, or, instead, included mainly physicians prescribing it (13). Usually the significance of a story emerges early in the interviewing or data-gathering process. It if does not, the writer abandons the story before he has too much work invested in a non-story.

Exceptions exist. For example, the significance of the diffuse electronic sensor development, mentioned earlier, did not emerge until very far along in the research. Sometimes the accumulated facts may show the writer a larger, more significant and more dramatic pattern than his sources see. Word of caution: Unless the writer is an expert himself, he should confirm this new and grander interpretation with expert sources. However, the writer should neither fear nor abandon this larger view. Additional sources will not hurt his story, since the single-source story, in general, lacks solidity. At least one scientist believes that science writers grasping for stories tend to underreach.

Planning the Story

The writer will need a plan for his story, whether he is writing a short news story or a full feature article, a newspaper story or a television-radio report. Determining the points of major significance, meaning and impact in a subject helps him form his story plan. However, this alone does not tell him how to write it. Each type of story demands a different plan, one tailored to fit each story's time, place and purpose. *Business Week* editors, for example, realize that a news section story (100 to 700 words, approximately) allows the writer only room enough to concentrate on one aspect of a story. The result: Forced sacrifice of secondary meanings, many details and subtleties. Other news magazines are forced into similar caricaturizations. Longer articles, such as cover stories or special reports, allow room for exploring almost all themes and angles.

John Noble Wilford, science writer for *The New York Times*, followed two totally different plans while reporting one story, the landing of the first astronauts on the moon (July 20, 1969) and their return to earth four days later. Under one plan he reported the flow of these events daily for his newspaper, more generous than most with its space. Simultaneously he was writing, also under another story plan, the final chapters of a 332-page book. The book appeared on the newsstands only four days after Astronauts Neil A. Armstrong, Edwin E. Aldrin, Jr., and Michael Collins returned (276). In the book, he followed a story plan set more than two years earlier to achieve a unified story amidst the rush of great events.

Story outlines traditionally form the writer's graphic "plan" for a story. Such a map, however, could just as well be sketched as the flow chart of the systems engineer or the experimenter's logic diagram. This outline represents the writer's decision about "What does it mean?" Here he sets out his main theme and chooses the pieces of his material. The proposed length, obviously, restricts the number of anecdotes, facts, etc., which the writer may build into his structure. Only the most essential pieces fit. Likely he will find he has 10 or even 100 times more material than he can use. He can take this as evidence of his thorough research; it will not be wasted. This storehouse of fact gives writers confidence in building their themes and in answering the inevitable questions their editors will ask.

Television requires even more precise planning than a print article. Early planning must have produced, for example, the segments of TV film or tape footage that will be integrated with the story. At the writing stage, the plan must allow the science writer to coordinate film clips, taped interviews and still pictures with the major points of his outline. Here is how Earl Ubell, science editor for WCBS-TV after leaving the *Herald Tribune,* describes it:

> From a simple typewriter pecker I have turned into producer, actor, film editor, director and picture scrounger. Not that I do all these jobs technically, but I must know enough about each of them to influence the quality of my stories. It is enormously hard work. I'm amazed at the high standards achieved under enormous pressures. Every edition is the last edition in television news. If you fail the first time, you have failed [265].

Limitations of time and space make planning a news story or TV news interview a short process. The writer has only one or two points to make. Writing and air time are similarly limited. But the demands for more unified news stories—those with a definite and rounded sequence of begining-middle-end, with a climax included—discourage merely starting to write and quitting when through. At the writing stage the great facts of science are so much lumber, mortar, bricks and steel the writer will assemble into a structured story.

Handling Story Elements

Journalism, particularly newspaper journalism, once demanded a "Five-W" beginning. This meant packing the who-what-when-where-and-why into the first few sentences. Editors now permit, even demand, more. The old Five-W beginning remains as serviceable as before, only why settle for this?

The *lead* opens the story. The writer hooks and holds the reader or viewer here or he has lost him to dozens of competing attractions. Competition includes other media, his family, his automobile, his recreation, his business and his daydreams.

Three science writers approached their story this way:

Minnesota has looked at the atom and found it partly evil.
　　　　　　　　　—Victor Cohn, *The Washington Post* (55)

Scientists at Houston's Manned Spacecraft Center have found a toxin in the Apollo 11 lunar sample which kills at least three strains of fairly hardy earth bacteria.
　　　　　　　　　—John Lannan, *Washington Star* (135)

Last July 28 Adolph (Rudy) Coniglio, who calls himself the best pizza maker in northern New Jersey, suddenly lost the ability to taste his food.
　　　　　　　　　—Stuart Auerbach, *The Washington Post* (14)

All contain elements of cosmic overview, variations of the factual Five-W opening, the scene-setting of dramatic fiction. And as fits most newspapers, the writers plunge from their lead right into the significance of their information. Magazines often allow a little more leisurely glide into the body of a story. Fred Warshofsky, who shared in a TV Emmy award for his scripting of science on *The 21st Century,* opened his story of the Apollo II discoveries with a capsuled 100-word history of the flight returning the first rock samples. The story appeared in Reader's Digest on the first anniversary of the flight. From this background opening, he launched into a story ticking off major discoveries drawn from the lunar rocks (275).

　　Each man chose the most eye-catching opening to hold the reader and carry him into the significance (What Does It Mean?) of the information following. Each could have opened, also, with quotes from news sources, with anecdotes or other material. But each chose his own way—as all writers must.

Now That You've Hooked Him...

Writers tear up dozens of leads, sometimes, before they hit the word combinations that they believe will catch a reader. Then comes the job of holding the reader while he is hauled to shore at the end of the story. The final version may be deceptive in its simplicity. The writer's outline or flowchart of topics should provide the sequence of events.

For years *The Wall Street Journal* has earned almost universal admiration for the way its editors and writers master the task of organizing material to haul the reader home.

Prof. Timothy W. Hubbard analyzes this success as the result of "an unusual and highly logical system of material organization" (105). He calls it the "DEE-system" of organization, remarkably well-suited for "trend" stories. Such "trend" stories aptly describe the effort of science writers to pin down advances of science, medicine, engineering and technology and their effect upon social, political and economic institutions as well. These are stories of change.

The DEE stands for *Description, Explanation* and *Evaluation.* Although the order of presentation is not frozen, it is logical, Professor Hubbard observes, to *describe* change first, *explain* a phenomenon and then *evaluate* its future.

Writers of the DEE persuasion must first identify the main theme or major thrust of the story for the reader clearly and plainly. And there must be one and only one main theme. Further, the reader must encounter this statement of significance very soon in the story; no wading through miles of description before he finds out why he is doing this.

Professor Hubbard cautions writers that a simplified DEE-system will not aid the writing of spot news, profiles of men and institutions and some political interpretations. However, the DEE-system, with variations, may aid the writer in sorting his material into manageable, functional blocks with a minimum of agonizing. And at the end, the reader must feel the writer has told him all he has set out to recount, that he has reached an end.

Guidelines for Writing

For the science writer at the keyboard is, in the end, the storyteller. He may be scientist, engineer or journalist; but here he becomes the ancient man beside an ancient campfire, recounting the tribal lore. He will find volumes and volumes on writing, if he chooses deeper exploration into the art of storytelling. All writers need *The Elements of Style* by William Strunk and E.B. White, in paperback. Fowler's *Modern English Usage* and Theodore M. Bernstein's *The Careful Writer* will help bail the writer out of most ordinary writing situations. *The Writer's Handbook,* published annually, offers many writing tips, a view of changing styles and current markets for stories.

Generally, the science writer continually reminds himself he is the translator, the clarifier, the simplifier of technical experience. He will keep his sentences short, and he seldom will pack more than one idea into a sentence. He will use specific, precise detail rather than general adjectives whose meanings have grown fuzzy.

He will write positively, confidently. Unless he does, neither the editor nor the reader will be convinced that he has a story worth telling. He will write in the active voice, avoiding the slow and passive verbs. He will make every effort that his command of language and sense of the dramatic can produce to cast his story in terms of human experience and to involve the reader with this new experience.

As a story teller he must move the reader along with his own enthusiasm and zeal. The story he tells is truly of his own making.

References

1. Abelson, Philip, *A Critical Appraisal of Government Research Policy,* The Robert A. Welch Foundation Research Bulletin No. 14 (Houston, Texas, 1963), pp. 1-17.
2. ____, "Science Reporting," *Science* (January 18, 1963), p. 127.
3. Abraham, Karl, Interview in New York (March, 1961).
4. ____, Interview in Houston, Texas (Summer, 1963).
5. Abramson, Rudy, "Lab Gains Spur Hopes for Peaceful Use of H-Energy " *The Washington Post* (July 5, 1970), p. 13.
6. Akagi, Akio, "Science in Japanese Newspapers and Television," *Understanding* 11 (Winter, 1963), p. 3.
7. Alsop, Joseph, and Alsop, Stewart, *The Reporter's Trade* (New York: Reynal and Company, 1958).
8. Ames Research Center news release No. 63-29 (July 11, 1963), quoting Donald K. Slayton, p. 1.
9. Andrepoulous, Spyros, "DNA Synthesis and Heart Transplants: Public Relations Aspects," *Archives of Surgery* (September, 1968), pp. 469-73.
10. *APN Newsletter* (undated), Novosti Press Agency, Puskin Square, Moscow, U.S.S.R., three packages (mimeographed) received in Spring, 1964.
11. Ashby, Eric, "Dons or Crooners," *Science* (April 8, 1960), pp. 1165-70.

12. Asimov, Isaac, *The Genetic Code* (New York: New American Library, 1962), pp. 1-181.
13. Auerbach, Stuart, "Doctors at Diabetes Centers Move to Refute NIH Study," *The Washington Post* (July 11, 1970), p. 3.
14. ____, "Loss of Taste Cured by Metal Treatment," *The Washington Post* (February 1, 1970), p. 1.
15. ____, "Moon Transmits Sound at Same Rate as (You Guessed It) Green Cheese," *The Washington Post* (July 25, 1970), p. 1.
16. Baker, W.O., *How Old Is the Age of Science?* The Robert A. Welch Foundation Research Bulletin No. 8 (Houston, Texas, 1961), p. 1-16.
17. Barrett, Edward W., Speech to students at Columbia University Graduate School of Journalism (Spring, 1961).
18. Barzun, Jacques, *Science: The Glorious Entertainment* (New York: Harper and Row, 1963), pp. 16-142.
19. Beckmann, J.A., M.D., Interview in his office (October, 1960).
20. "The Bell is Ringing," *Time* (May 29, 1964), pp. 74-78.
21. Bender, William, Jr., "What Can You Tell the Press about a Newsworthy Patient?" *Medical Economics* (February 27, 1961), pp. 136-41.
22. ____, "When Your Patient Makes the Headlines," *Medical Economics* (February 7, 1961), p. 142.
23. Billard, Jules, "Tabular Breakdown of Active Members," *NASW Newsletter* (June, 1964), p. 16.
24. Bird, Robert S., "Metropolitan Proves Warrior Figures Fake," *The New York Herald Tribune* (February 14, 1961), p. 1.
25. Bishop, Jerry, Interview in New York (December 26, 1960).
26. ____, "Surgeons and Stock Markets," *NASW Newsletter* (December, 1963), p. 32.
27. Blakeslee, Alton (as told by Earl Ubell), "Covering the News of Science," *The American Scientist* (December, 1957), p. 330.
28. ____, "Science Writing," *Editor and Publisher* (August 13, 1960), p. 75.
29. Blakeslee, Mrs. Howard W., Personal letter to author with NASW membership list for 1964.
30. Boland, Mrs. Moselle, "Modern Art in Nature," *Texas Magazine*, Supplement to *The Houston Chronicle* (March 1, 1964), p. 10-11.
31. ____, "Symptons Are Chills, Nausea," *The Houston Chronicle* (August 21, 1964), p. 8.

32. Boring, Edward G., "Comments on Teleology," *Science* (March 6, 1959), pp. 609-10.

33. Borman, Frank, "The Expanding Role of the Pilot in Space Exploration," Speech at American Institute of Aeronautics and Astronautics, Los Angeles, California (June 17, 1963).

34. Brandenburg, George A., "Ruth Moore Covers Man, Past and Present," *Editor and Publisher* (September 10, 1961), p. 44.

35. ____, "Snider Covers Science Beat with Distinction," *Editor and Publisher* (November 26, 1960), p. 43.

36. Bureau of the Budget, *Special Analysis: Budget of the United States* (Washington, D.C.: Government Printing Office).

37. Burkett, Warren, "Biologist Hunts Giant Molecules That May Hold Secret of Mental Health," *The Houston Chronicle* (February 27, 1964), Sec. 4, p. 1.

38. ____, "Body Chemical May Shed Light on Cancer," *The Houston Chronicle* (November 18, 1964), p. 1.

39. ____, "Brain Drain No Problem," *The Houston Chronicle* (February 27, 1964), Sec. 4, p. 1.

40. ____, "Cinderellas of Science," *The Houston Chronicle* (September 14, 1964), Sec. 2, p. 8.

41. ____, "City Mosquitoes Spread Encephalitis," *The Houston Chronicle* August 21, 1964), p. 9.

42. ____, "MSC Starts Surgery to Save World's Largest Space Chamber," *The Houston Chronicle* (September 24, 1964), Sec. 6, p. 1.

43. ____, "1968 Big Year," *The Houston Chronicle* (September 1, 1963), p. 5.

44. ____, "Ranger Flight Has Simplified Moon Shot," *The Houston Chronicle* (August 9, 1964), Sec. 3, p. 8.

45. ____, "Showdown at the Mohole," *The Houston Chronicle* (May 15, 1963), p. 1.

46. ____, "Texas Targets Will Test Astronaut Eyes," *The Houston Chronicle* (May 3, 1965), p. 12.

47. ____, "There's More Going On in Science," *Quill* (May, 1970), pp. 16-19.

48. ____, "To: Senator Goldwater; Subject: Military in Space," *The Houston Chronicle* (July 23, 1964), Sec. 4, p. 2.

49. "Burned Beauty," *Time* (December 9, 1961), p. 67.

50. "Business in 1961: Automation Speeds Recovery, Boosts Productivity, Pares Jobs," *Time* (December 29, 1961), p. 50.

51. Chevalier, Lois M., "Do Science Writers Raise False Hopes?" *Medical Economics* (April 13, 1959), pp. 69-71.
52. Clarke, Alfred E., "Research Urged into Sweeteners," *The New York Times* (September 10, 1964), p. 30.
53. Cohn, Victor, "Are We Really Telling the People about Science?" *Science* (May 7, 1965), pp. 750-53.
54. ___, "NSF in Line for Big Increase in Funds for Basic Research," *The Washington Post* (July 11, 1970), p. 2.
55. ___, "Public Fights A-Power," *The Washington Post* (October 19, 1960), p. B-1.
56. ___, "Science's Sharpening Conscience," *Technology Review* (February, 1970), pp. 12,13.
57. ___, "Science Writer Ethics," *NASW Newsletter* (September, 1960), pp. 11-13.
58. ___, "A Science Writer's View," *AAAS Bulletin* 7, no. 1, p. 4.
59. *Communications and Medical Research,* Proceedings of a national symposium of the University of Pennsylvania in Philadelphia (October 17, 1964), pp. 1-90.

Abelson, Philip	17-19
Blakeslee, Alton	60
Cant, Gilbert	63
Farber, Sidney	12
Flanagan, Dennis	14-16
Fraley, Pierre	65-66
Shannon, James A.	25,40
Snider, Arthur J.	71
Steven, William P.	27-31,41-42
Sullivan, Walter	74
Ubell, Earl	32,36,39

60. *Constitution of the National Association of Science Writers* (Port Washington, New York), pp. 1-10.
61. Contract No. BG 751-86-5-7, Manned Spacecraft Center, Houston, Texas, 1964.
62. Crawford, J.H., "Editorial," *Applied Physics Letters* (November 1, 1962), p. 52.
63. Dart, John, "The Sixth W—'So What?' " *Quill* (May, 1970), pp. 12-14.
64. Davis, Watson, "The Challenge of Science Coverage," *Quill* (October, 1963), pp. 15-16.

65. ____, "Hucksters in the Temple," *NASW Newsletter* (June, 1963), p. 17.

66. Dietz, David, "Billionth of a Second Clocked by Physicists," *The New York World Telegram and Sun* (March 25, 1961), p. 6.

67. Dorozynski, Alexander, "Clearing It Up about Relativity," *Columbia University Forum* (Summer, 1960), pp. 14-18.

68. ____, "Russia, with Love," *NASW Newsletter* (June, 1964), p. 25.

69. "Dr. Hutschnecker's Plan," *Newsweek* (April 20, 1970), p. 76.

70. Edelson, Edward, "How Long, Cold Winters Produced Hitler," *The Washington Post* (June 7, 1970), p. 3, *Book World*.

71. Einstein, Albert, 1933 letter of resignation from Prussian Academy of Sciences. In *Ideas and Opinions*, edited by Carl Selig (New York: Crown Publishers, 1964), p. 207.

72. "FAA to Tell Crash Cause," *The New York World Telegram and Sun* (June 23, 1961), p. 207.

73. Faget, Maxime, "The Moon . . . and Beyond," *Texas Magazine,* supplement to *The Houston Chronicle* (May 31, 1964), pp. 58-59.

74. Fesperman, Tom, "Science News Notes," *NASW Newsletter* (March, 1963), p. 45.

75. Flesch, Rudolph, *How to Write, Speak, and Think More Effectively* (New York: The New American Library, 1963).

76. Foster, John, *Science Writer's Guide* (New York: Columbia University Press, 1963).

77. Fraley, Pierre, *Annual Report (1963) of the Council for the Advancement of Science Writing* (Phoenixville, Pennsylvania, 1963).

78. ____, "The Education and Training of Science Writers," *Journalism Quarterly* (Summer, 1963), pp. 323-25.

79. ____, Mimeographed notice of availability of a science writer's research post at National Tuberculosis Association laboratory at the University of Colorado, Boulder, Colorado (Summer, 1964).

80. ____, "Should Science Writers Be Scientists," *NASW Newsletter* (March, 1963), pp. 21-23

81. Friedman, Rick, "Doctors and Reporters Treat Problems of Science in News," *Editor and Publisher* (March 20, 1965), pp. 9, 46.

82. "Gag on News Is Seen in U.S. Ethics Codes," *The New York Times* (August 2, 1961), p. 15.

83. Gail, Harry R., "The AAAS Meeting," *NASW Newsletter* (March, 1961), p. 4.

84. Geiger, H. Jack, and Berg, Roland, "Science, the Press, and the Citizens," Mimeographed report (Port Washington, New York: 1958).

85. Glass, Bentley, "The Academic Scientist 1940-1960," *Science* September 2, 1960), pp. 603-04.

86. "Goldwater Charges LBJ Misused Data," *The Houston Post* (September 20, 1964), p. 12.

87. Goudsmit, S.A., "Publicity," *Physical Review Letters* 4, no. 1, p. 5.

88. Gould, Jack, "Radio Problem," *The New York Times* (April 16, 1961), Sec. X, p. 15.

89. Grant, Mary, Interview with former Palo Alto, California, science writer in New York (April, 1962).

90. Griffin, Alan, "Censorship," *The World Book Encyclopedia* 3 (1955), p. 1304.

91. "A Guide to Careers in Science Writing," Mimeographed report (Port Washington, New York: NASW, 1963).

92. Haseltine, Nate, "Bugs, Bug Juice, and World," *NASW Newsletter* (June, 1963), p. 36.

93. ____, "Editor's Page," *NASW Newsletter* (September, 1964), p. 40.

94. Heintze, Carl, "Hinterlands Science," *NASW Newsletter* (December, 1963), p. 33.

95. Hildebrand, Joel, *Science in the Making* (New York: Columbia University Press, 1957).

96. Hill, Arthur R., "Coming Down the Mountain," *NASW Newsletter* (March, 1963), p. 37.

97. Hillaby, John, "Game Harvesting for Food is Urged," *The New York Times* (September 1, 1961), p. 20.

98. Hohenberg, John, Interview in New York concerning Robert Dwyer, his contemporary who died in 1961 (Fall, 1961).

99. ___ , *The Professional Journalist* (New York: Henry Holt and Company, 1960).

100. Holton, Gerald, "Modern Science and the Intellectual Tradition," *Science* (April 22, 1960), pp. 1187-89.

101. "Hospital Code for Press Relations," *NASW Newsletter* (March, 1961), pp. 31-33.

102. Hotz, Robert, "Editorial," *Aviation Week* (March 9, 1964), p. 11.

103. ____, "Editorial," *Aviation Week* (June 15, 1964), p. 21.

104. ____, "Editorial," *Aviation Week* (August 3, 1964), p. 11.

105. Hubbard, Timothy, "Anatomy of Excellence," *Columbia Journalism Review* (Fall, 1968), pp. 31-33.

106. "Impact of an Astronaut," *Twentieth Review of Operations: January 1-June 30, 1963* (Washington, D.C.: USIA, 1963), pp. 12-15.

107. International Atomic Energy Agency, Vienna datelined press release detailing debate (September 28, 1961).
108. Jackson, Lura S., "Washington Round-Up, or How to Beat the Army." *NASW Newsletter* (December, 1960), pp. 32-34.
109. Jaffe, Bernard, *Michelson and the Speed of Light* (Garden City, New York: Doubleday and Company, 1960), pp. 1-173.
110. Janson, Donald, "Farm Migrants' Jobs Dwindle as Use of Machinery Advances," *The New York Times* (February 28, 1961), p. 46.
111. Jeans, James, *The Growth of Physical Science* (New York: Premier Books, 1958), p. 240.
112. Johnson, Earl J., "The Realities of World News Editing" Sixteenth Annual William Allen White Memorial Lecture at The University of Kansas in Lawrence, Kansas (February 10, 1965), pp. 1-15.
113. Johnson, Kenneth G., "Dimensions of Judgment of Science News Stories," *Journalism Quarterly* (Summer, 1963), pp. 315-22.
114. Johnsrud, John, "Old Idea Yields New Appliances," *The New York Times* (June 28, 1961), p. 43.
115. Jones, David E.H., "The Stability of the Bicycle," *Physics Today* (April, 1970), pp. 34-40.
116. Joravsky, David, "The Lysenko Affair," *Scientific American* (November, 1962), pp. 41-49.
117. "Journalism Education and Social Science Journalism," *Understanding* (Fall, 1964), p. 5.
118. Justice, Blair, "As Limitless As the Stars," *The Texas Press Messenger* (January, 1963), pp. 10-11.
119. ____, "A Few Words about Wordage," Speech at a science news conference at The University of Texas, Austin, Texas (November 27, 1961).
120. ____, "Loud Silence on the 4th," *The Houston Post* (July 4, 1964), p. 2.
121. ____, "Scientists Can Be Key to Very Rapid Economic Growth," *The Houston Post.*
122. Karp, Walter, "Searching for Science," *Columbia University Forum* (Spring, 1965), pp. 12-16.
123. Kearl, Bryant, "Russian Science Writing," *Understanding* (March, 1964), p. 1.
124. Keller, Rev. James, "Your Stake in Space Flights," *New York Mirror* (July 17, 1961), p. 17.
125. Kone, Eugene, Mimeographed guide to operation of press rooms at American Institute of Physics meetings (1962).

126. ____, Official announcement of William L. Laurence dinner by the American Institute of Physics, New York (1964).

127. Kranish, Art, "White House Committee Seeks Science Newspaper," *Washington Science Trends* (October 4, 1965), p. 1.

128. Krieg, Margaret, *Green Medicine* (New York: Rand, McNally and Company, 1964), pp. 1-463.

129. Krieghbaum, Hillier, "Public Interest in Science News," *Science* (April 24, 1959), pp. 1092-95.

130. ____, *Science, the News, and the Public* (New York: New York University Press, 1958).

131. Kusch, Polykarp, Address to 1961 Pulitzer Prize jury in New York.

132. ____, Interview in New York (February, 1962).

133. ____, "Science Doesn't Have All the Answers," *The New York Herald Tribune* (April 12, 1961), Sec. 2, p. 3.

134. Lannan, John, "DuBridge Defends U.S. Science Policy," *Washington Star* (July 16, 1970), p. 3.

135. ____ "Toxin Found in a Sample of Moon Dust," *Washington Star* (March 11, 1970), p. 1.

136. Lear, John, "The Fourth of July," *The Saturday Review* (July 4, 1964), pp. 38-40.

137. ____, "The Trouble with Science Writing," *Columbia Journalism Review* (Summer, 1970), pp. 30-34.

138. Leger, Richard R., "They Said It Couldn't Be Done, But Mr. Jones Has Almost Done It," *The Wall Street Journal* (April 3, 1970), p. 1.

139. Leonard, Jonathan, "Science Fiction," *Time* (April 3, 1964), pp. 48-49.

140. Lepkowski, Wil, "Odd Meson Upsets Physicists," *The Houston Post* (August 7, 1964), Sec. 2, p. 5.

141. Lessing, Lawrence, "The Three Ages of Science Writing," *Chemical and Engineering News* (May 6, 1963), pp. 88-91.

142. Letter in author's files.

143. Lieberman, J. Ben, and Kimball, Penn T., "Educating Communicators of Specialized Subjects," *Journalism Quarterly* (Autumn, 1961), pp. 527-34.

144. Loory, Stuart, "NIH and the People's Right to Know," *NASW Newsletter* (March, 1964), pp. 28-31.

145. Lubell, Samuel, *When People Speak* (New York: Opinion Reporting Workshop, Graduate School of Journalism, Columbia University, 1960).

146. Makino, Takuji, Interviews at author's home and a Manned Spacecraft Center in Houston (September, 1963).

147. Mann, Martin, "President's Page," *NASW Newsletter* (September 1964), p. 2.

148. "Manned Spacecraft Center Information Procedures for Contractors, Suppliers, and Vendors," Mimeographed (Houston, Texas, 1964).

149. Manned Spacecraft Center Release No. 63-122, distributed to Houston, Texas, newsmen (October, 1963).

150. Markel, Lester, Speech at Columbia University Graduate School of Journalism (Spring, 1961).

151. "The Master Technicians," *Time* (November 27, 1964), pp. 95-98.

152. McCallister, Ralph, and Brown, Diana (eds.), National Conference for Scientific Information (New York: Scientists Institute for Public Information, 1964).

153. McCarthy, Eugene, "Science News in Kitchener," *NASW Newsletter* (September, 1963), pp. 46-47.

154. McLeod, Jack M., and Swinehart, James W., *Satellites, Science, and the Public* (Ann Arbor: University of Michigan Survey Research Center, 1959), pp. 1-57.

155. Meyer, Philip, "Detroit: When Scholars Joined Journalists," *Columbia Journalism Review* (Fall, 1967), p. 10.

156. Milne, Donald S., "Science Writing Down Under," *NASW Newsletter* (March, 1964), p. 33.

157. Montague, Joseph Franklin, M.D., "The New Style Hypochrondiac," *Clinical Medicine* (September, 1966), p. 7.

158. Morrison, Harriet, "Science Invades the Home Field," *The New York Herald Tribune* (January 10, 1961), p. 16.

159. Mosher, Charles A. Broadcast recorded in Washington, D.C. for Ohio radio stations (October 27, 1963).

160. Murray, J. Edward, "The Crisis of Meaning," *Editor and Publisher* (February 4, 1961), p. 7.

161. *NASA Authorization: 1964*, Transcript of hearings, Subcommittee on Manned Space Flight (Washington, D.C.: Government Printing Office, 1963), Document 96-504.

162. *NASW Fact Sheet* (Port Washington, New York, 1964).

163. National Academy of Sciences, *Technology: Processes of Assessment and Choice* (Washington, D.C.: Government Printing Office, 1969), p. 163.

164. National Academy of Engineering, *A Study of Technology Assessment* (Washington, D.C.: Government Printing Office, 1969), p. 208.

165. National Aeronautics and Space Act of 1958, Public Law 85-568 (72 Stat. 426; 42 U.S.C. 2451) (Washington, D.C.: Government Printing Office), Document 75923.
166. National Science Foundation, *Federal Funds for Research, Development, and Other Scientific Activities* (Washington: National Science Foundations, 1969), p. 280.
167. ____, *Federal Support to Universities and Colleges* (Washington: National Science Foundation, 1969), p. 89.
168. ____, *National Patterns of R&D Resources 1953-70* (Washington: National Science Foundation, 1969), p. 26.
169. ____, *R&D Activities in State Government Agencies* (Washington: National Science Foundation, 1967), p. 68.
170. ____, *Research and Development in Industry* (Washington: National Science Foundation, 1969), p. 110.
171. Negus, Sydney S. "Report on Public Information Activity," *Science* (February 17, 1961), pp. 488-90.
172. Nelson, Harry, "Minutes of the 1964 Winter Meeting." *NASW Newsletter* (March 1965), pp. 4-6.
173. Newman, James R., "Experiments Toward a Humor of Science," *Scientific American* (September, 1964), pp. 243-45.
174. "Obscenity OK If It's Science," *The Houston Chronicle* (March 26, 1964), p. 1.
175. O'Leary, Ralph, Letter to author (Spring, 1962).
176. "One Hundred Top News Events Listed for 1961," *The New York Times* (December 31, 1961), p. 6-E.
177. Organisation for Economic Cooperation and Development, *Reviews of National Science Policy* (Paris, 1968), p. 600.
178. Osmundsen, John A., "Scientists Find Genetic Roots in a Host of Diseases," *The Washington Post* (June 14, 1970), p. B-1.
179. O'Toole, Thomas, "Lack of Sleep a Factor at Kent?" *The Washington Post* (May 17, 1970), p. 4.
180. Overuse of Artificial Sweeteners Assailed," *The Wall Street Journal* (September 9, 1964), p. 6.
181. Page, Irvine H. M.D., "Ethics and the Press," *NASW Newsletter* (March, 1969), p. 16.
182. Perlman, David, Interview at Columbia University Graduate School of Journalism (Spring, 1961).
183. ____, "Our Peripatetic Correspondent," *NASW Newsletter* (September, 1964), pp. 27-29.

184. "Physicist, 43, in Defense Science Post," *The New York Herald Tribune* (March 10, 1961), p. 8.

185. Piel, Gerard, *Science in the Cause of Man* (New York: Alfred A. Knopf, Inc., 1961).

186. Plumb, Robert K., "Scientist Defines Electricity Anew," *The New York Times* (April 21, 1961), p. 27.

187. Porter, Russell, "President Urges Press to Censor News Aiding Reds," *The New York Times* (April 28, 1961), p. 1.

188. Porterfield, Bill, "Women Who Are Busts as Brains Probably Have Other Endowments," *The Houston Chronicle* (August 30, 1964), p. 1.

189. *The Practical Values of Space Exploration*, House Report No. 1276 (Revised, 1961) (Washington, D.C.: Government Printing Office) Document No. 75756, pp. 1-40.

190. President's Task Force on Science Policy, *Science and Technology: Tools for Progress* (Washington, D.C.: Government Printing Office, 1970), p. 48.

191. Press release from the American Association for the Advancement of Science (Washington, D.C., September 24, 1964).

192. Price, Don K., "Escape to the Endless Frontier," *Science* (May 7, 1965), pp. 743-49.

193. ____, "Organization of Science Here and Abroad," *Science* (March 20, 1959), pp. 760-65.

194. Randal, Judith, "Biomedical Headline-Grabbing," *The Washington Star* (December 9, 1971), p. A-12.

195. ____, "Doctors Should Caution 'Pill' Users," *Evening Star* (January 8, 1970, p. 6.

196. Raymond, Jack, "McNamara Acts to Block Leaks in Security Data," *The New York Times* (May 11, 1961), pp. 1, 14.

197. Reed, James, "Cooperation, a Two-Way Street," *Editor and Publisher* (September 17, 1960), p. 55.

198. "Report of the Committee on Science in the Promotion of Human Welfare," *Science* (July 8, 1960), pp. 68-70.

199. "Reporting News of Medicine," *Editor and Publisher* (August 13, 1960), p. 75.

200. Response to query by Manned Spacecraft Center officials in Houston, Texas, on Contract No. NAS 9-1396.

201. Riesel, Victor, "Inside Labor," *The New York Mirror* (April 14, 1961), p. 32.

202. Rivers, Caryl, "Good Reporters Make Best Science Writers," *Editor and Publisher* (January 23, 1965), p. 17.

203. Rostand, Jean, "Popularization of Science," *Science* (May 20, 1960), pp. 1491-95.
204. Rourke, Francis E., *Secrecy and Publicity, Dilemmas of Democracy* (Baltimore, Maryland: Johns Hopkins Press, 1961).
205. "Russia Uses More Science than U.S.," *The Record* (Hackensack, New Jersey, April 7, 1962), p. 2.
206. Scheer, Julian, Unclassified TWX message to all NASA public affairs officers (October 1963).
207. Schmeck, Harold M., Jr., "Computer Is Used in Fight on Pests," *The New York Times* (March 19, 1961), p. 128.
208. ____, "Egeberg Expects Aware Patients," *The New York Times* (May 6, 1970), p. 5.
209. ____, "Wound in Head Ended Hope of Saving Kennedy," *The New York Times* News Service as published in *The Houston Chronicle* (September 28, 1964), p. 13.
210. Schramm, Wilbur, *Science and the Public Mind* (Washington, D.C.: American Association for the Advancement of Science, 1962), pp. 1-20.
211. Schreiber, Edward, and Anderson, O.D., "Properties and Composition of Lunar Materials: Earth Analogies," *Science* (June 26, 1970) p. 1579.
212. "Science in the Kitchen," *The Sciences* (February 1, 1964), p. 6.
213. "Science Link to Defense under Study," *The New York Herald Tribune* (March 6, 1961), p. 2.
214. "Science Scoop," *Understanding* (Spring, 1964), p. 1.
215. Scientist, Meet the Press (Philadelphia, Pennsylvania: Smith, Kline and French Laboratories, 1964), pp. 1-16.
216. "Scientists Assays Scholar's Schism," *The New York Times* (April 18, 1961), p. 39.
217. "Scoop Happy," *Newsweek* (June 19, 1961), p. 95.
218. Seaman, Barbara, Letter in the *NASW Newsletter* (December, 1969), p. 30.
219. Sears, Paul B., *Through the Language Barrier,* Transcript of a science news workshop, edited by John Meehan (Louisville, Kentucky: University of Louisville, February 8-9, 1960).
220. Shelton, William, Interview with editorial director for World Book Science Service, Houston, Texas (Summer, 1964).
221. Sherburne, E.G., "Science on Television," *Journalism Quarterly* (Summer, 1963), pp. 300-05.
222. Siminovitch, L., "The Synthesis of DNA: A Success Story—and a Moral," *Science Forum* (April, 1968), pp. 25-26.

223. "Simulated Satellite Interceptions Are Claimed," *The Houston Post* (September 19, 1964) p. 4.

224. Slosson, Edwin E., and Davis, Watson, *How Science Service Covers the Science Front* (Washington, D.C.: Science Service, 1962).

225. Small, William E., "The Science Writer Survey," *NASW Newsletter* (December, 1964), pp. 11-15.

226. Smith, Betty Stuart, "Chemist Aids Cold Sterilization Research," *The Christian Science Monitor* (March 17, 1961), p. 10-C.

227. Smith, Jack, Interview at Columbia University, New York (Spring, 1961).

228. ____, "Step Right Up and Meet New Members," *NASW Newsletter* (June, 1963), p. 45.

229. Snider, Arthur J., "Frills of Science," *Understanding* (Summer, 1964), p. 2.

230. Snow, C.P., *The Two Cultures and the Scientific Revolution* (New York: Cambridge University Press, 1961), pp. 1-42.

231. Soule, Gardner, "College Sheepskin May Be Tomorrow's Union Card," *The New York World Telegram and Sun* (June 22, 1961), p. 21.

232. Spencer, Mildred, "Minutes of the December Meeting," *NASW Newsletter* (March, 1964), p. 5.

233. Steven, William P., Speech at a science news conference at The University of Texas, Austin, Texas (November 28, 1961).

234. Stewart, Ileen E., and McGurl, Vincent, "Dues and Membership in Scientific Societies," *Science* (October 7, 1960), p. 939.

235. Stokely, James, "Professional Training," *NASW Newsletter* (September, 1964), pp. 18-20.

236. Strassmann, Erwin O., M.D., Letter to Bureau of Accuracy and Fair Play, *The Houston Chronicle* (September 10, 1964).

237. ____ "Physique, Temperament, and Intelligence in Infertile Women," *International Journal of Fertility* 9, No. 2, pp. 297-301.

238. "Stratoscope Results," National Science Foundation press release (Washington, D.C., June 28, 1964).

239. Strother, Robert S., "He Measured the Speed of Light," *Readers Digest* (July, 1964), pp. 193-200.

240. Suchy, John T., "Larsen's ABCs of Research," *NASW Newsletter* (September, 1963), pp. 31-33.

241. Sullivan, Walter, An advisory to Turner Catledge, managing editor of *The New York Times* (April 20, 1961).

242. ____, Air Found Gaining in Carbon Dioxide," *The New York Times* (September 11, 1961), p. 29.

243. ____,"Camera Records Satellite Lights," *The New York Times* (September 9, 1961), p. 17.

244. ____, "Science: Desalting Water," *The New York Times* (June 28, 1964), Section E, p. 7.

245. ____, "Scientists Adrift on Arctic Isle Find a Flourishing Plant Life," *The New York Times* (October 17, 1961), p. 41.

246. ____, "Volcano's Effect on Life Is Studied," *The New York Times* (September 23, 1961), p. 21.

247. ____ "Writing Science for the Public," *Physics Today* (August, 1970), pp. 51-53.

248. "Supersonic A-ll Unveiled," *Aviation Week* (March 9, 1964), p. 16.

249. Swanson, Charles E., "What They Read in 130 Daily Newspapers," *Journalism Quarterly* (Fall, 1955), p. 411 *ff*.

250. Szent-Gyorgyi, Albert, Paper delivered at Robert A. Welch Foundation Conference, Houston, Texas (November 18, 1964).

251. Talese, Gay, *The Kingdom and the Power* (New York: NAL-World, 1969), pp. 4-7.

252. Taylor, Raymond L., "A Report on the Eighth New York Meeting," *Science* February 17, 1961), pp. 472-75.

253. Teller, Edward, "Secrecy: No Longer a Security Asset," *Public Affairs*, reprinted in *The Wall Street Journal* (July 15, 1970), p. 12.

254. Thistle, M.W., "Review of N.A.S.W. Surveys," *Science* (February 27, 1959), pp. 458-59.

255. Thomson, Sir George, "The Two Aspects of Science," *Science* (October 14, 1960), pp. 996-98.

256. Toth, Robert C., Interview in Washington (August 5, 1965).

257. ____, "When Should the Taxpayer Be Told?" *NASW Newsletter* (March, 1963), p. 17.

258. Troan, John, "Science Writing Today and Tomorrow," *Science* (April 22, 1960), pp. 1193-96.

259. Turner, Joseph, "A Distinction That Needs Elaborating," *Science* (January 5, 1961), p. 3445.

260. "Two Anti-Satellite Systems," *The Houston Chronicle* (September 18, 1964), p. 1.

261. Ubell, Earl, "Aids to the Science Writer," Speech at a Conference on Science and the Press at The University of Texas, Austin, Texas (November 27-29, 1961).

262. ____, "Child Killer May Be Ruled Sane," *The New York Herald Tribune* (February 28, 1961), p. 1.

263. ____, "The Mass Media and the Image of Science," Speech to the Thomas Alva Edison Foundation Conference in Washington, D.C. (November 6, 1964).

264. ____, NASW-NASA Liaison," *NASW Newsletter* (September, 1963). pp. 12-13.

265. ____, *NASW Newsletter* (December, 1966), p. 2.

266. ____, "Proton and Neutron Cores Photographed," *The New York Herald Tribune* (February 2, 1961), p. 3.

267. ____, "Take Fear, Hate; Stir; Result: Mob," *The New York Herald Tribune* (May 24, 1961), p. 6.

268. "U.S. Curbs News on Missile Tests," *The New York Times* (April 22, 1961), p. 12.

269. "U.S. To Curb Data About Satellites," *The New York Times* (February 11, 1961), p. 21.

270. Van Dellen, Theodore, M.D., "Science Helps the Housewife," *The Houston Chronicle* (May 8, 1964), p. 24.

271. Van Dyke, Vernon, *Pride and Power: The Rationale of the Space Program* (Urbana, Illinois: University of Illinois Press, 1964).

272. Vineberg, Dusty, "Covering Medicine," *Editor and Publisher* (August 13, 1961), p. 38.

273. Wade, Nicholas, "Scientists and the Press: Cancer Scare Story That Wasn't," *Science* (November 12, 1971), pp. 679-80.

274. Waife, S.O., Letter from the AMWA secretary-treasurer, Indianapolis, Indiana (April, 1961).

275. Warshofsky, Fred, "What the Moon Rocks Reveal," *Reader's Digest* (August, 1970), pp. 157-64.

276. Wilford, John N., *We Reach the Moon* (New York: Bantam Books, 1970), p. 332.

277. Willard, Bradford, "Science Reporting," Letters to the Editor, *Science* (July 29, 1960), p. 1306.

278. Winter, Arthur, M.D., "My Wife the Science Writer," *NASW Newsletter* (September, 1967), p. 24.

279. Wise, David, "2 Unofficial Emissaries of Kennedy Paved Way to Free RB-47 Flyers," *The New York Herald Tribune* (March 13, 1961), p. 1.

280. Witcover, Jules, "Surliest Crew in Washington," *Columbia Journalism Review* (Spring, 1965), pp. 11-15.

281. Wolfle, Dael, "Author's Choice," *Science* (May 8, 1959), p. 1247.

282. Woodbury, David O., "Shotgun Wedding of Science and Humor," *NASW Newsletter* (June, 1964), p. 22.
283. "World Watches U.S. Science," *Twentieth Review of Operations: January 1-June 30, 1963* (Washington, D.C.: USIA, 1963), pp. 36-40.
284. Wykert, John, "Shrink Woo-in Lays an Egg," *NASW Newsletter* (March, 1968), p. 27.
285. Yu, Frederick T.C., ed., *Behavioral Sciences and the Mass Media* (New York: Russell Sage Foundation, 1968), p. 270.
286. Yuncker, Barbara, "Has Talk of Fats Reached Saturation Point?" *The New York Post* (July 13, 1961), p. 2.

Appendix

Awards of Science Writing

Recognition encourages human endeavor. Medals, money and certificates are used to reward outstanding performance in all fields and professions, and journalism is no exception. Science writers are eligible for most of the major prizes offered in newspaper journalism, magazine writing, radio and television broadcasting. Science writers also may participate in a variety of grants and fellowships that encourage further study. The amount may well come to more than $50,000 annually for those competitions open to science writers' stories; a complete tabulation of all prizes is impossible because of the large number of purely local and state awards. The American Medical Association, for example, encourages state and local associations to establish awards for writers and broadcasters at their levels in addition to the national AMA awards.

The amount of these awards varies. Sometimes local awards convey a certificate of recognition and a few dollars for an honorarium. Usually the sponsoring organization will pay the expenses of the winning writer, or a representative of his publication to attend the presentation ceremony. Depending on the wealth of the sponsors, however, many of these local awards may bring the author several hundred dollars. Sponsorship varies. In New York, the state health department and the veterinary medical society are among those giving journalism awards. Often an industry or a trade association sponsors journalism awards for stories relating to a special field. Journalistic organizations award prizes also; both the Texas Headliners Club in Austin and the Los Angeles Press Club have bestowed cash prizes upon authors of science stories. The National Association of Science Writers has considered establishing its own journalism awards in addition to the ones given at the annual meeting of the American Association for the Advancement of Science, where the NASW holds its annual meeting.

Writers should remember that a certain amount of skepticism attends the awarding of prizes. Beyond normal competitive spirit, which must suffer in any engagement where there are winners and losers, awards in journalism sometimes carry unflattering implications. Some awards, none of them in science writing specifically, were designed to garner publicity for the sponsor's products, services or name. Other sponsors go to great lengths to disassociate the selection of a reward from their organizations' special economic, political or professional interests; the sponsors acknowledge, however, that the possibility exists that writers, editors and producers may pay more than ordinary attention to a topic because of the added incentive. Generally, the final selection of an award winner is made by a panel of experts, including some editors and writers.

Policy in respect to awards varies. Some publications will not enter contests or allow their staff writers to do so. Others permit writers to accept awards, but not cash, from organizations on their regular news coverage assignments. Often the publication will pay the writer the amount of money he would have received under less stringent rules for avoiding conflict of interest. On the other hand, many publications feel that winning awards enhances the reputation of the writer and his publication. Often the publication or station has a promotion director who attempts to see that printed and broadcast material is entered in all possible competitions.

Sometimes the writer knows his material is entered, sometimes not. Some publications regard competitions so highly that the company matches any award money won by its writers.

It is safe to assume that few writers consciously set out to write specifically for the awards, however; the reputation for being a "scalphunter" is not one to cultivate among peers. To be realistic, competition for awards that carry enough money to make the effort worthwhile is so keen and the selection so subjective that the odds for crafting a story specifically as a prize winner are very low. For example, thousands of science writers followed the story of man's landings on the moon; various Project Apollo stories or series naturally occurred to thousands of writers. All scientific, engineering and human aspects of the flights were covered thoroughly. Yet, Jerry Bishop of *The Wall Street Journal* won a $1,500 award in 1972 for his profile of a single lunar rock and its meaning to scientists. Or how could C.P. Gilmore predict that his *Popular Science* (April, 1969) report on the possibility of earthquake prevention would win the 1970 American Institute of Physics–U.S. Steel Foundation award? Most science writers pursue the stories that interest them or their editors. Winning an award merely confirms their original good judgment.

Following is a selection of national awards and their sponsors. Some reward science and medical writing only; others are more general but have been won regularly by science writers. Since rules and entry deadlines are always subject to change, the writer should contact the sponsor for current requirements. Some contests award separate prizes for radio, television and print media; other awards are limited, even to certain types of printed media. Because awards and division are always shifting, the writer will want to consult the sponsor's most recent guidelines. Encyclopedic listings of all writing awards can be found in the *Editor and Publisher Yearbook*, available at most libraries.

Multimedia Awards

Print, TV and Radio

American Cancer Society (219 East 42nd Street, New York, New York 10017): Awards given through state and metropolitan divisions of the American Cancer Society.

American Medical Association, Medical Journalism Committee (535 N. Dearborn Street, Chicago, Illinois 60610): $1,000 each in newspaper, magazine, editorial writing, radio and television categories.

American Optometric Association, Public Service Awards (7000 Chippewa Street, St. Louis, Missouri 63119): $500 each in newspaper, magazine and television.

Arches of Science Award, Pacific Science Foundation (200 Second Avenue North, Seattle, Washington 98109): $25,000 for science communication; usually given to prominent scientist for popularizing science.

Arthritis Foundation (1212 Avenue of the Americas, New York, New York 10036): Three awards of $1,000 each in the Russell L. Cecil contest for outstanding writing about arthritis in newspapers, magazines and broadcasting.

Aviation/Space Writers Association (101 Greenwood Avenue, Jenkintown, Pennsylvania 19046): $100 to $500 in 14 divisions for efforts in newspapers, trade publications, general magazines, photography, television, radio, books, public relations and government information dissemination.

Bradford Washburn Award, Boston Museum of Science (Science Park, Boston, Massachusetts 02114): $5,000 for efforts contributing to increased understanding of science by laymen.

Deadline Club Awards (Deadline Club Chapter of Sigma Delta Chi, c/o George B. Bookman, New York Stock Exchange, 11 Wall Street, New York, New York 10005): $500 each in various categories of journalism; awards often won for science writing.

The Forum Award, Atomic Industrial Forum (850 Third Avenue, New York, New York 10022): $1,000 for press, radio, television, film or other publication.

George Polk Memorial Awards (Department of Journalism, Long Island University, Zeckendorf Campus, Brooklyn, New York 11201): Citations for outstanding writing, reporting and editing in all media.

James T. Grady Award, American Chemical Society (Public Relations Department, 1155 Sixteenth Street NW, Washington,

D.C. 20006): $1,000 for science writing in chemical subjects; open for all media.

Howard W. Blakeslee Awards, American Heart Association (44 East 23rd Street, New York, New York 10010): $500 each for varying number and types of media awards for articles on heart disease.

Kalinga Prize, United Nations Educational and Scientific Organization (UNESCO House, Place de Fontenoy, Paris 7-e, France): $20,000, approximately but varies; usually given to scientist who devotes extraordinary amount of effort in helping public understanding.

Albert Lasker Medical Journalism Awards, Lasker Foundaation (866 United Nations Plaza, New York, New York 10017): $2,500 each in newspaper, magazine and broadcast journalism for articles on current medical problems.

Morse Writers Award, Committee on Public Information, American Psychiatric Association (1700 Eighteenth Street NW, Washington, D.C. 20009): $200, approximately, noncompetitive "token" for contribution to understanding of psychiatry.

Highway Users Federation, Alfred P. Sloan Awards for Highway Safety (200 Ring Building, Washington, D.C. 20036): $7,500 single staff award for service to highway safety plus plaques in 20 media divisions.

National Conservation Award for Communications, National Wildlife Federation (Executive Director, 1412 Sixteenth Street NW, Washington, D.C. 20036): $1,000 for article or broadcast script which aids understanding of foundation's goals.

National Media Award, American Psychological Association (1200 Seventeenth Street NW, Washington, D.C. 20036): $1,000 each for print and broadcast divisions.

Sigma Delta Chi Awards in Journalism (35 E. Wacker Drive, Suite 3108, Chicago, Illinois 60601): Citations in 16 categories; prestige awards conferred by journalism professionals.

TWA Annual Writing and Picture Competition (Trans World Airlines, Inc., 605 Third Avenue, New York, New York 10016): $100 awards in approximately 12 divisions; subjects of commercial aviation, air travel.

Print Media Awards

AAAS–Westinghouse Science Writing Awards, American Association for the Advancement of Science (1515 Massachusetts Avenue NW, Washington, D.C. 20005): $1,000 each for newspapers over and under 100,000 and general magazines.

AIP-U.S. Steel Foundation Science Writing Award in Physics and Astronomy (335 East 45th Street, New York, New York 10017): $1,500 award for article or series in print medium.

American Dental Association, Science Writers Awards Committee (211 East Chicago Avenue, Chicago, Illinois 60611): $1,000 each for newspaper and magazine stories on dental care and research.

American Newspaper Guild, Heywood Broun Award (1126 Sixteenth Street NW, Washington, D.C. 20036): $1,000 for newspaper or magazine journalism: guild membership not required.

Bell Awards, National Mental Health Association (10 Columbus Circle, New York, New York 10023): Plaque for daily and weekly newspapers and two popular books.

Claud Bernard Science Journalism Award, National Society for Medical Research (1330 Massachusetts Avenue NW, Washington, D.C. 20005): $1,000 each for newspapers over and under 100,000 and general magazines.

Edward J. Meeman Awards for Conservation, Scripp-Howard Foundation (200 Park Avenue, New York, New York 10017): $1,000 for newspaper articles on subject of land conservation and practices.

G.M. Loeb Awards, University of Connecticut (Storrs, Connecticut 06268): $3,000 each for newspapers, magazines, columns-editorials; prime interest in business and financial journalism.

John Hancock Awards for Excellence, John Hancock Mutual Life Insurance Company (200 Berkeley Street, Boston, Massachusetts 02117): $1,500 for magazine and newspaper articles, but must have business or financial significance.

Journalism Awards, American Osteopathic Association (212 East Ohio Street, Chicago, Illinois 60611): $300 in three divisions.

Journalism Awards for Family Health Care, American Academy of General Practice (Volker Boulevard and Brookside, Kansas City, Missouri 64112): $2,000 divided among first, second and third placings.

Journalism Award, American Society of Anesthesiologists (515 Busse Highway, Park Ridge, Illinois 60068): $900 divided among three placings.

National Book Awards, National Book Committee (1 Park Avenue, New York, New York 10016): $1,000 for science book among five qualifying categories.

National Headliners Club Awards in Journalism (National Headliners Club, Convention Hall, Atlantic City, New Jersey 08401): Citations for writing in assorted journalism divisions.

National Magazine Awards (Columbia University School of Journalism, Columbia University, New York, N.Y. 10027): five awards for excellence in magazine journalism including reporting, public service and specialized publications.

National Society of Professional Engineers (2029 K Street NW, Washington, D.C. 20006): $1,000 awarded for article dealing with any phase of engineering.

PBK Award in Science (Phi Beta Kappa, 1811 Q Street NW, Washington D.C. 20009): $2,500 for scientist's contribution to literature or science.

Penney-Missouri Awards (School of Journalism, University of Missouri, Columbia, Missouri 65201): $1,000 magazine award in each of several home-oriented divisions including health.

Public Affairs Awards, American Political Science Association (1527 New Hampshire NW, Washington, D.C. 20036): Citation and trip to APSA in Washington for reporting on any phase of state and local government.

Pulitzer Prizes (Pulitzer Awards Director, Graduate School of Journalism, Columbia University, New York, New York 10027): $1,000 each for various divisions of newspaper and wire service writing.

Rychener Memorial Award, American Association of Opthalmology (1100 Seventeenth Street NW, Washington, D.C. 20036): $250 for newspaper or magazine article on eyes or vision.

Stokes Conservation Award, Stokes Award Committee (1346 Connecticut Avenue NW, Washington, D.C. 20036): $500 newspaper award for conservation article or series.

Worth Bingham Prize, Worth Bingham Memorial Fund (3400 Reservoir Road NW, Washington, D.C. 20007): $1,000 award for newspaper or magazine reporting on situation of national significance where public interest is ill-served.

Broadcast Awards

Alfred I. DuPont and Columbia University (Graduate School of Journalism, Columbia University, New York, New York 10027): Citation for outstanding broadcast journalism; neither format nor categories frozen.

Emmy Awards, National Academy of TV Arts and Sciences (New York, New York): Citations in almost bewildering number of categories for which science material may be used.

UCLA-Dumont Award (Graduate Department of Journalism, University of California at Los Angeles, Los Angeles, California 90024): $5,000 for excellence in basic issues shown by a TV journalist.

Study and Fellowships

Strictly speaking, the person who receives a fellowship or grant or internship is not being rewarded for his past excellent performance. In practice, however, such awards are looked upon as recognition of his good work and his potential to benefit from further study or experience. When the Sloan-Rockefeller Advanced Science Writing Program at Columbia University closed in 1970, after 10 years, the major program devoted exclusively to advanced science writers closed also. However, its example has encouraged the development of academic programs and similar fellowships in several universities. The science journalist will find several other programs which offer him opportunities for broadening his experience.

AAAS-Science *Magazine*: Working internship in science and public policy on the weekly journal of the largest scientific society (Office of the Editor, *Science*, 1515 Massachusetts Avenue NW, Washington, D.C. 20005).

AIP Seminars: Educational seminars for journalists, lasting one or two days, led by experts in scientific fields (American Institute of Physics, Eugene Kone, 335 East 45th Street, New York, New York 10017).

Alicia Patterson Fund Fellowship Program: One-year travel and study fellowships abroad after five years' experience (535 Fifth Avenue, New York, New York 10017).

American Cancer Science Writers Seminar: Week-long briefing on new results of cancer research, held each year in a different city (American Cancer Society, 219 East 42nd Street, New York, New York 10017).

Council for the Advancement of Science Writing: For scientists and journalists entering science writing, the CASW offers a broad self-tutoring program, under guidance of experienced science writers and several topical seminars each year (Executive secretary Henry A. Goodman, 201 Christie Street, Leonia, New Jersey 07605).

Distinguished Scholars' Program, Cranbrook Institute of Science: Residency program to help institutes interpret science to public through various mediums (The Director, Cranbrook Institute of Science, Bloomfield Hills, Michigan 48013).

Mental Health Information Program: Tuition and living allowances in a two-year program leading to masters degree (Newhouse Communications Center, School of Journalism, Syracuse University, Syracuse, New York 13210).

Nieman Fellowships: Tuition plus family living allowances for academic year to experienced journalists; science writers eligible for general participation, and one fellowship, sponsored by the Arthur D. Little Foundation, is designated especially for science writers (Director, Nieman Programs, Harvard University, Cambridge, Massachusetts 02134).

NIH-Information Intern Program: Working internship in National Institute of Health information and education activities (Director of Public Information, National Institute of Health, Bethesda, Maryland 20014).

Public Affairs Fellowship Program: Working experience and study in public policy fields (American Political Science Association, 1527 New Hampshire Avenue NW, Washington, D.C. 20036).

Training and Research Program in Science Writing: Experience-study program at graduate level with university information office (James A. Larsen, News and Publication Service, Bascom Hall, University of Wisconsin, Madison, Wisconsin 53706).

Fund for Investigative Journalism: Finances, travel and expenses for special investigations connected with abuses of public trust, including drug regulations, medical practice, etc. (Attn. James P. Boyd, 2933 Ordway NW, Washington, D.C. 20008).

Trans-Action Fellowships: Working internship preparing social science articles for publication in semipopular magazine (*Trans-Action* magazine—now called *Society* magazine—Irving L. Horowitz, editor-in-chief, Rutgers, The State University, New Brunswick, New Jersey 08903).

Washington Journalism Center: Sponsored by the Kiplinger Family Foundation, the center offers a variety of fellowship and internship arrangements for journalists interested in federal operations (Washington Journalism Center, 2000 G street N.W., Washington D.C. 20026).

Science Writing Associations

American Medical Writers Association (420 Lexington Avenue, Suite 417, New York, New York 10017)

Council for Advancement of Science Writing (201 Christie Street, Leonia, New Jersey 07605)

International Science Writers Association (c/o Gordon Rattray Taylor, The Hall, Freshford Bath, Somerset, England)

National Association of Science Writers (Post Office Box H, Sea Cliff, New York 11579)

Index

Abelson, Philip H., 29, 91, 134, 156
Abraham, Karl, 28
Abramson, Rudy, 14
Accuracy, 44, 46, 52-54, 85, 86, 93, 94, 98, 124, 127, 139-141, 152, 176
A-11, 152
Alicia Patterson Fund, 208
Alsop, Joseph and Stewart, 155
American Association for Advancement of Science, 17, 30, 40, 43, 53, 65, 81, 101, 133
American Association of Opthalmology, 207
American Broadcasting Companies (ABC), 98
American Cancer Society, 19, 208
American Chemical Society, 20 173, 203
American Heart Association, 204
American Institute of Physics, 17, 19, 38, 91, 133, 202
American Medical Association, 15, 43, 68, 71, 143, 203
American Medical Writers Association, 4, 18, 209
American Newspaper Guild, 205
American Optometric Association, 203

American Osteopathic Association, 206
American Physical Society, 40, 82
American Political Science Association, 206
American Psychiatric Association, 204
American Psychological Association, 204
American Society of Anesthesiologists, 206
American Sociological Association, 40
Anderson, Jack, 155
Andreopoulous, Spyros, 128
Antiballistic missile, 16, 153
Antartic, 19
Antiscience, 121
Applied science, 34, 108
Army, 142, 143, 168-72
Arthritis Foundation, 203
Arthur D. Little Foundation, 208
Arts, 106
Asimov, Isaac, 40
Associated Press, 18, 26, 27, 91, 114
Atomic Energy Commission, 20, 145
Atomic Industrial Forum, 203
Auerbach, Stuart, 136, 179

209

Aviation/Space Writers Assocation, 4, 203
Aviation Week, 151, 152, 153
Awards in science writing, 79, 200-09

Background in science writing, 21, 47, 66, 67
Baker, W.O., 33
Baltimore Sun, 115
Barrett, Edward W., 114
Barzun, Jacques, 38
Bell Telephone Laboratories, 32
Bender, William, 129
Bengelsdorf, Irving, 59
Bergman, Jules, 98
Bicycles, 136
Billard, Jules, 111
Bishop, Jerry, 108, 109, 202
Blakeslee, Alton, 3, 26, 114
Blakeslee, Howard, 18
Boland, Moselle, 103, 105
Boring, Edward G., 42
Borman, Frank, 122
Boston Globe, 30, 115
Boston Museum of Science, 203
Boston University, 40
Bribery attempted, 3
Broadcasting, 21, 98, 99, 107, 117, 178, 179, 202, 203
Brown, Harold, 14
Brown University, 40
Bulletin of the Atomic Scientists, 114
Business news, 108, 109
Business Week, 71, 175, 177

Cameras, 76-78
Cancer and virus, 31, 44
Cant, Gilbert, 124
Career advancement, 115
Charlotte Observer, 30
Chicago Daily News, 36, 37, 41, 47, 97, 114
Chicago Sun Times, 74, 111
Christian Science Monitor, 110, 115
Cincinnati Enquirer, 98, 112

Classified information, 151, 155
Cleveland Press, 18
Codes of ethics, 129-131
Cohn, Victor, 2, 10, 34, 79, 90, 126, 129, 143, 144, 179
Columbia University and Graduate School of Journalism, 21, 24, 63, 114, 206, 207
Commando tactics, 164-167
Competition, 98
Conference papers, uses, 82, 87
Conflict of interest, 25, 120
Content versus enterprise, 43, 45
Contracts, 159, 164
Controlling news, 26, 27, 75, 82, 88, 119-23, 129, 162
Conventions, 81-102
Council for Advancement of Science Writing (CASW), 18, 23, 24, 47, 62-64, 67, 68, 208, 209
Cowen, Robert, 115
Cranbrook Institute of Science, 208
Crediting sources, 134
Criticisms of science writing, 29, 30, 46, 79, 80, 92
Cromie, William J., 65
Cuba, Bay of Pigs, 148

Dart, John, 175, 176
Davis, Watson, 19, 122, 127
Deadline Club, 203
Decision makers, 26
Defense Department, 20, 163
Detroit Free Press, 21
Detroit News, 19
Dietz, David, 18
Distortion of science, 28
Dorozynski, Alexander, 136, 138
Drugs, 31, 127, 128
DuBridge, Lee A., 156
DuPont, E.I. de Nemours, 11
Dwyer, Robert 18

Edelson, Edward, 57
Einstein, Albert, 125
Electronic battlefield, 168, 172-76
Employment in science, 10
Endorsement in ads, 126

Environmental Protection Agency, 20
Etzioni, Amitai, 24

Fads in science, science writing, 31, 44, 124
False hopes, raising, 30, 44, 127
Family Health, 115
Federation of American Societies for Experimental Biology, 81
Fesperman, Thomas G., 30
First publication rights, 31, 133
Flanagan, Dennis, 45
Flesch, Rudolph, 75
F-111, 153
Food and Drug Administration, 3
Foster, John, 63
Fraley, Pierre, 18, 62, 67
Freedom of information, 143, 144
Freelance writing, 107, 114, 115
Fund for Investigative Journalism, 209
Funding of science, 9, 10, 11, 35

Gagarin, Yuri, 125
Geiger, H. Jack, 59
Generalists, 63, 64
Gillette, Jean, 30
Gilmore, C.P., 202
Glass, H. Bentley, 12
Goldwater, Barry, 153, 171
Goodman, Henry A., 23, 63
Greenberg, Daniel, 136
Growth in science, 12

Harvard University, 38, 42, 58
Haseltine, Nate, 125
Health, Education, and Welfare, Department, 15, 24, 145
Heintze, Carl, 112
Hildebrand, Joel, 32, 43, 124
Highway Users Federation, 204
Hill, Arthur R., 113
Hines, William, 142
Hohenberg, John, 21, 28
Holton, Gerald, 38
Hospital codes, 131
Hotz, Robert, 151-54

Houston Chronicle, 21, 103, 139, 129
Houston Post, 21, 59, 64
Hubbard, Timothy W., 180
Humor, 135-38
Hutschnecker, Arnold, 24

Informed patients, 127
International Atomic Energy Agency, 15
International News Service, 59
International projects, 13, 38, 149
International Science Writers Association, 209
Interviews, 90

Japan, 56, 57
John Hancock Mutual Life Insurance Company, 205
Johnson, Earl J., 4
Johnson, Kenneth G., 53
Johnson, Lyndon B., 15
Johnson, Virginia E., 140
Johnsrud, John, 11
Joravsky, David, 40
Joule, James Prescott, 40
Journals, use of, 35, 36, 65, 66, 82
Junkets, 19, 127
Justice, Blair, 59, 66, 105, 135

Kaempffert, Waldemar, 18
Kalinga Prize, 41
Karp, Walter, 32
Kearl, Bryant, 55
Kennedy, John F., 14, 57; School of Government, 8
Kennedy, Robert, 22
Khrushchev, Nikita, 14
Kimball, Penn T., 63
Kiplinger Family Foundation, 209
Knight Newspapers, 24
Kornberg, Arthur, 76
Kranish, Art, 116
Krieghbaum, Hillier, 49, 63, 124
Kusch, Polykarp, 16, 29, 123

Lal, Gobind Behari, 18
Lannan, John 156, 179

Larsen, Carl, 137
Lasker Foundation, 204
Lear, John, 30, 135
Laurence, William L., 18, 58, 132
Lederberg, Joshua, 54
Leonard, Johathan, 54
Lepkowski, Wilbert, 96, 143
Lewis, Howard, 71
Lewis, Richard, 114
Lessing, Lawrence, 172, 173
Lieberman, J. Ben, 63
Limitations of science, 123
Linder, Lee, 91
Local scientists, 96
Lochbaum, Jerry, 79
Loory, Stuart, 115, 145, 147
Los Angeles Times, 14, 26, 115, 133, 176
Lysenko, Trofim D., 40

Manhattan Project, 12
Markel, Lester, 33
McCormack, Mike, Congress, 16
McElheny, Victor K., 30
McGraw-Hill, 96, 115, 143, 169, 171
McNamara, Robert S., 147
McNutt, Wilbourn, 28
Mann, Martin, 115
Marwick, Charles, 128
Masters, Dr. William H., 140
Medical Economics, 129
Medical World News, 128
Medicine, 91, 103, 106, 128-30, 174
Menzies, Ian, 115
Meyer, Philip, 24
Michigan State University, 60
Misunderstanding, science and medicine, 124
Montreal Star, 105
Moore, Ruth, 74, 111
Mosher, Congressman Charles A., 136
Moss, Congressman John E., 148, 172
Murray, J. Edward, 21

National Academy of Sciences–National Academy of Engineering–National Research Council, 2, 3, 30, 82, 143
National Aeronautics and Space Administration, 68, 78, 90, 109, 121, 133, 145, 157
National Association of Science Writers, 3-6, 17, 19, 28, 33, 42, 47, 59-62, 84, 88, 111, 115, 125, 128, 131, 137, 143, 209
National Book Committee, 206
National Bureau of Standards, 68
National Geographic, 111
National Headliners Club, 206
National Institutes of Health, 20, 46, 145-47, 176, 209
National Magazine Awards, 206
National Mental Health Association, 205
National Research Council of Canada, 26
National Science Foundation, 2, 9, 10, 15, 20, 35, 68
National Society for Medical Research, 205
National Society of Professional Engineers, 206
National Wildlife Federation, 204
Nature, 65
Newark (N.J.) Star Ledger, 128
News, defined, 22, 32, 95, 123
News, judging, 97
New media, 117
New York Daily News 57
New York Herald Tribune, 18, 44
New York Times, 11, 18, 21, 22, 25, 26, 30, 33, 46, 57, 58, 77, 101, 110, 114, 132, 140, 148, 155, 177
New York University, 49
Nieman Fellowships, 208
Nixon, Richard, 2, 14, 15
Nobel Prizes, 16, 36, 123

O'Leary, Ralph, 64
Operations Research Society, 16

"Operators" in science, 91
Organization for Economic Co-operation and Development (OECD), 9

Pacific Science Foundation, 203
Parkinson's Disease, 26
Pearson, Jean, 19
Perlman, David, 101, 174
Phi Beta Kappa, 206
Philadelphia Bulletin, 21, 28
Piel, Gerard, 25
Pittsburgh Press, 115
Plumb, Robert K., 91
Politics in science, 8, 13, 15, 16
Pooling news coverage, 78
Popularization of science, 38-40, 46, 47, 53, 57, 75,
Popular Science, 202
Potter, Robert D., 18
Prematurity in reporting, 44
Press conferences, 88
Press-government conflict, 147
Pressrooms, 86
Price, Don K., 8, 12, 13
Proxmire, Senator William, 171
Psychology Today, 24
Publicity seeking, 30, 31, 91
Public relations, 19, 27, 43, 71, 76, 80, 82, 84-86, 88, 91, 112, 127, 132, 149, 150, 154, 157-64.
Pugwash Conference, 15
Pulitzer Prizes, 18, 29, 58, 206
Pure science, 3, 4, 108
Purposes of science writing, 31, 37-39, 41

Randal, Judith, 31, 127
Readings in science, 62
Readership of science news, 33, 48-53, 75, 178, 179
Release times, 88
Restraint by science writers, 30, 44
Reuters, 26
Riesel, Victor, 12
Rochester (Minnesota) Post Bulletin, 114

Rockefeller Institute, 68
Rosenfeld, Albert, 115
Rostand, Jean, 41
Rostow, Walter W., 14
Rourke, Francis E., 157
Russia, 36, 40, 54, 55, 125, 148

San Angelo (Texas) Standard Times, 30
San Antonio Express and News, 79
San Francisco Chronicle, 101, 174
Saturday Review, 30
Scheer, Julian, 145
Schmeck, Harold M., 57, 110
Schoenfield, Allen, 18
Schools and science, 23, 52
Schramm, Wilbur, 50
Science, 5, 29, 42, 65, 91, 133, 134
Science advisor, 156
Science Digest, 114
Science in government, 7
Science meetings, 116
Science news, 22, 23, 32-38, 45, 95
Science newspaper, 115
Science Service, 18, 73
Science Trends, 116
Science writers defined, 3, 17, 18, 20
Scientific American, 25, 45, 65
Scientists in congress, 16
Scripps Howard Newspapers, 18, 118; Foundation, 205
Seaman, Barbara, 128
Sears, Paul B., 37
Secrecy, 148, 149
Security, 2, 77, 120, 145
Sensationalism and nonsensationalism, 30, 31, 54, 138-40
Sex and science, 27, 139, 140
Shannon, James, 46
Sheehan, Neil, 155
Sherburne, E.G., 53
Sigma Delta Chi, 204
Significance in news, 30, 53, 73, 97, 176
Simons, Howard, 115, 155
Sloan-Kettering Institute for Cancer Research, 20

Small city newspapers, 30, 111-14
Small, William E., 60
Smith, Betty Stuart, 110
Smith, Jack, 98, 112
Smith, Kline and French, 84, 92
Smithsonian Institution, 101
Smoking and cancer, 118-20
Snider, Art, 36, 41, 97, 114
Snow, Sir Charles, 37
Society, 24
Sociology, 24, 59
Specialization, 21, 22, 107-10
Spencer, Mildred, 128
Spencer, Steven M, 127
Sports, 105
SR-71, 152
Stanford University, 54, 128
Steven, William P., 47, 64, 129
Stokes Award Committee, 207
Stokley, James, 59
Story guidelines, 72-74
Story types, 69-70
Sullivan, Walter, 22, 30, 31, 64, 77,
    101, 109, 114
Syracuse University, 208
Szent-Gyorgyi, Albert, 36

Tannenbaum, Percy, 52
Teller, Edward, 148
Thistle, M.W., 26
Thomson, George P., 34
Timing stories, 71, 83, 88
Toth, Robert C., 133, 144
Trade journals, 38, 82, 165
Training for science news writing,
    24, 30, 58-68
Trans-Action fellowships, 208
Transplants, 71
Trans World Airlines, 204
Troan, John, 28, 42, 68, 115, 118,
    172
Texas University, 104

Ubell, Earl, 21, 27, 44, 47, 59, 66,
    74, 104, 141, 144, 178

United Nations, 15, 41; Educa-
    tional and Scientific Organiza-
    tion, 204
United Press International, 4, 18,
    26
United States Information Agency,
    20, 149, 150
US Steel Foundation, 202
University of California, 174, 207
University of Connecticut, 205
University of Michigan, 49
University of Missouri, 206
University of Wisconsin, 52

Van Dyke, Vernon, 157
Vietnam, 8, 15, 155, 168
Vineberg, Dusty, 105
Violence, 1, 22-25, 57, 59
Vivian, Congressman Weston E., 16

Wallace, Weldon, 115
Wall Street Journal, 108, 109, 116,
    140, 141, 180, 202
Warshofsky, Fred, 179
Washington Post, 2, 10, 26, 34, 90,
    115, 125, 155, 177, 179
Washington Star, 31, 127, 156, 179
Wayne State University, 24
WCBS-TV, 21, 178
Weiner, Norbert, 16
Westbrook, J.H., 124
Westinghouse Award, 79, 155
Wiesner, Jerome, 15
Wilford, John N., 177
Winter, Dr. Arthur, 128
Winter, Ruth, 128
Witcover, Jules, 154
Wolfe, Dael, 133
Women's pages, 106
Woodbury, David O., 138
Worth Bingham Memorial Fund,
    207
Writing guides, 155, 156, 174-81
Wykert, John, 24

Yale University, 37
Young, Lewis, 175